Elite • 95

OSPREY
PUBLISHING

World War II Medal of Honor Recipients (2)

Army & Air Corps

S Sinton & R Hargis • Illustrated by R Bujeiro

First published in Great Britain in 2003 by Osprey Publishing
Elms Court, Chapel Way, Botley, Oxford OX2 9LP, United Kingdom
Email: **info@ospreypublishing.com**

ISBN 1 84176 614 3

CONSULTANT EDITOR: Martin Windrow
Editor: Anita Hitchings
Design: Alan Hamp
Index by Glyn Sutcliffe

Originated by Electronic Page Company, Cwmbran, UK
Printed in China through World Print Ltd.

03 04 05 06   10 9 8 7 6 5 4 3 2 1

A CIP catalog record for this book is available from the British Library.

FOR A CATALOG OF ALL BOOKS PUBLISHED BY
OSPREY MILITARY AND AVIATION PLEASE CONTACT:
Osprey Direct UK, P.O. Box 140, Wellingborough, Northants, NN8 2FA, UK
E-mail: **info@ospreydirect.co.uk**

Osprey Direct USA, c/o MBI Publishing
P.O. Box 1, 729 Prospect Ave, Osceola, WI 54020, USA
E-mail: **info@ospreydirectusa.com**

www.ospreypublishing.com

Artist's note

Readers may care to note that the original paintings from which the
color plates in this book were prepared are available for private
sale. All reproduction copyright whatsoever is retained by the
Publishers. All enquiries should be addressed to:

Ramiro Bujeiro, C.C.28, 1602 Florida, Argentina

The Publishers regret that they can enter into no correspondence
upon this matter.

Photographer's note

The color photographs on page 33 were taken by Richard Boucher
of New York.

MEDAL OF HONOR RECIPIENTS (2) ARMY & AIR CORPS

In 1904, the Medal of Honor was redesigned as a gilt five-pointed star with the bust of Minerva in the center. The medal was often called the "Gillespie" Medal after its designer, Civil War veteran George Gillespie. At the same time, the ribbon was changed to the now-familiar light blue with 13 white stars. When full-size medals were not worn with uniform, the light blue ribbon (with only five stars showing) was worn on the ribbon bar. (National Archives and Records Administration – NARA)

THE MEDAL OF HONOR

AFTER THE UNION ROUT at Bull Run in the summer of 1861, Northern morale was at a very low point, and the War Department proposed the first military decoration for bravery since the short-lived Purple Heart of George Washington's time. However, Winfield Scott, General-in-Chief of the Army, dismissed the idea. The Navy Department took the lead and on December 21, 1861, a "medal of honor" was approved for Navy enlisted men.

With the departure of Gen. Scott, legislation was introduced in Congress to authorize an Army medal of honor for "such noncommissioned officers and privates as shall most distinguish themselves by their gallantry in action, and other soldier-like qualities, during the present insurrection." This legislation took effect in July 1862, and in March 1863, eligibility for the medal was extended to officers and it was made a permanent award.

The design of the medal was patterned after the Navy medal approved several months before. This design was a two-inch bronze five-pointed star in the center of which stood a female figure representing Minerva, holding aloft a shield. At her right was a crouching figure holding serpents that appeared to be slinking off at the sight of Minerva. This central motif was surrounded by 34 stars. The Army design replaced the Navy anchor suspension with an eagle above crossed cannon. The ribbon was blue at the top and striped red and white below. The medal remained in this form until 1896, when the ribbon was changed to red/white/blue vertical stripes.

In 1904, the Army changed the design of the medal itself. The new composition, created by General George Gillespie, himself a Medal of Honor recipient in the Civil War, retained the five-pointed star shape, but added an enameled wreath behind the star. The eagle with spread wings remained but the cannon were replaced with a plaque displaying the word "VALOR". In this version, all metal was gold rather than bronze and the ribbon was changed to the familiar light blue with 13 white stars.

In 1918, at the end of World War I, Congress reviewed military medals and established graduated awards. As a result, the Distinguished Service Cross and the Silver Star were instituted. (Other awards, such as the Bronze Star, ranking just below the Silver Star, were added during World War II.) Now gallantry not rising to the level required for award of the Medal of Honor could be adequately recognized. At the same time, the standards for the Medal of Honor were restated to emphasize the exalted place of the nation's highest decoration. From then on, the medal would be awarded for "gallantry and intrepidity at the risk of life above and beyond the call of duty." The Medal of Honor had come into its own as the ultimate symbol of military gallantry for the American fighting men.

MEDAL OF HONOR RECIPIENTS

By World War II, the Medal of Honor was usually worn suspended by a ribbon worn around the neck. Occasionally, it is worn on the ribbon bar in the spot of priority. (NARA)

ARMY

First Lieutenant Willibald C. Bianchi

In December 1941, two major US forces posed a threat to Japanese plans for expansion into South East Asia and Indonesia: the Navy's Pacific fleet at Pearl Harbor and the combined American-Philippine Army in the Philippine Islands. The latter had a strength, at least on paper, of 130,000 men, under the command of General Douglas MacArthur. Any Japanese expansion in Asia was certain to run up against these forces, so the Japanese called for their rapid destruction. On December 8, one day after the attack on Pearl Harbor, the Japanese Air Force raided Clark Field in the Philippines and destroyed the majority of Gen. MacArthur's air power while it was still on the ground.

This raid was only the first step in the Japanese offensive against the Philippines; invasion and complete subjugation of these islands was the ultimate goal. On December 10 and 12, preliminary landings by the Japanese, aimed at securing airfields in support of the main landings planned for December 22, occurred at the northern and southern ends of the island of Luzon, northwest of the capital, Manila. General Masaharu Homma would lead the invasion force, consisting of units of the Japanese 14th Army, ashore at Lingayen Gulf. The Japanese discounted the fighting ability of the units of the six-year-old, but largely untrained, Philippine Army and planned a speedy victory over the outnumbered Americans of the US Army's Philippine Division.

According to the American War Plan Orange, US forces were to be deployed north of Manila in an attempt to contain any Japanese invasion and conduct fighting down the length of the island of Luzon. Other units of the Philippine-American Armies were to strengthen control of Manila Bay and the fortress islands that defended it. In the event, Japanese landings to the south of the American defense line on December 24 disrupted Gen. MacArthur's plans and forced the defenders to abandon Manila and retreat into the Bataan peninsula.

In December 1941, First Lieutenant Willibald C. Bianchi served as a member of the 45th Infantry of the Philippine Division, a unit of the regular US Army made up of the 43rd, and three other infantry regiments, which had been in the Philippines since 1920. These regiments had left their enlisted personnel at home, however, and thus the Philippine Division (approximately one-half were Philippine

Scouts) was composed of native Philippine soldiers commanded by regular US Army officers and noncommissioned officers. As war approached, the Scouts were augmented with engineers, cavalry, and field artillery. Trained to high standards and recently equipped with modern US Army gear, the Scouts were expected to give a good account of themselves when the time came. "Bill" Bianchi, a farm boy from Minnesota, was one of them, assigned as a new lieutenant in the 45th Infantry after graduation from South Dakota State University in 1940.

Initially, the 45th Infantry was held in reserve on Luzon until Japanese intentions became clear. As the invasion unfolded, the Philippine Division fought a series of delaying actions as they were pushed southwards. By the last week in January 1942, Lt. Bianchi and his men were in defensive positions near the southern end of the Bataan Peninsula in the "Reserve Battle Position", a line that stretched from the town of Bagac in the west to Orion in the east. On January 25, Lt. Bianchi volunteered to lead a platoon of Scouts in an attack on Japanese machine gun positions.

Lt. Willibald Bianchi was a regular Army officer attached to the Philippine Scouts of the US Army's Philippine Division. At least two other members of the Philippine Scouts received the Medal of Honor in the first months of the war, Second Lieutenant Alexander Nininger (see page 59) and Mess Sergeant Jose Calugas, who dashed across a shell-swept field to rescue one of his battery's guns from the advancing Japanese on Bataan. (NARA)

The attack was to be supported by some M3 Stuart tanks, of dubious value against dug-in Japanese positions in the jungle. When early in the action Bianchi was hit in the hand by Japanese machine gun fire, he threw his rifle aside and advanced with only a pistol, using cover to work his way into close range. When he was within 20yds or so of the machine gun position, he left cover and tossed a hand grenade into the machine gun nest, putting it out of action, but not before he was wounded twice in the chest. Unable to walk, Lt. Bianchi pulled himself onto one of the knocked-out Stuart tanks and began firing the turret-mounted machine gun until knocked unconscious by the concussion from a Japanese grenade.

Lt. Bianchi recovered from his wounds, but for him and the other self-proclaimed "Battling Bastards of Bataan", the long ordeal of Japanese captivity was about to begin. When the Bataan Field Force was ordered to lay down their arms in April 1942, some 76,000 became prisoners of the Japanese. Lt. Bianchi became invaluable to the men on the three-day Death March to the prisoner-of-war camps where inhuman conditions awaited them. Japanese discipline, harsh even to its own soldiers, was monstrous when applied to prisoners of war, who had committed the shameful act of surrender.

Lt. Bianchi organized the prisoners and kept up morale. Since he was a trusted officer, Lt. Bianchi was placed in charge of food rationing, often going short himself so that more needy comrades received the extra food they needed to survive. For almost three years, Bianchi endured the rigors of being a prisoner of war. Then, after the Allies began the reconquest of the Philippines in October 1944, Lt. Bianchi and several hundred other prisoners were crowded aboard a Japanese merchant ship to be taken back to Japan as forced labor. On January 9, 1945, the ship came under fire from American aircraft unaware that

American POWs were aboard. The ship was sunk by a direct hit and all aboard were lost.

After the war, Lt. Bianchi's mother, Carrie, accepted the Medal of Honor her son was awarded during a small private ceremony. Later she showed her patriotism when she wrote, "I am proud to be able to give to this generation and to our beloved America the most precious gift that life makes possible, my only son."

Colonel William Hale Wilbur

In 1942, Allied prospects for eventual victory were at their lowest ebb. America had suffered disasters at Pearl Harbor and the Philippines, the British had lost the fortress of Singapore, the Dutch Antilles had fallen, and Australia was threatened. In Europe, Poland and France had fallen, Soviet Russia had been penetrated all the way to Stalingrad, and in North Africa, the *Afrika Korps* threatened Egypt and the Suez Canal. Stalin was so hard pressed he demanded action in the West to relieve pressure on the beleaguered Soviet Army. The Western powers were willing to accede to Stalin's demand but opinion was divided on the proper place for the "Second Front" invasion to take place; the British favored the Mediterranean coast to coordinate with the British 8th Army fighting in North Africa. The Americans, especially Fleet Admiral E. J. King and General George Marshall, backed a cross-Channel invasion of France on the Cotentin Peninsula. Eventually, agreement was reached and Vichy-French controlled territory in North West Africa was chosen.

The operation, code-named TORCH, called for the landing of three task forces of some 60,000 American and British troops in a wide zone, from Safi on the Atlantic coast of Morocco east to Algiers on the Mediterranean coast. The mission of these troops was twofold: first, to cut off Axis supplies to the *Afrika Korps* and, second, to bring Vichy-controlled French forces stationed in Africa back into the war on the Allied side.

Allied commanders were uncertain as to the nature of the reception that they would receive at the hands of the defending Vichy French. When France was overrun by the Germans in 1940, an armistice was cobbled together, leaving the still unoccupied portions of the country and all its dependencies overseas in the

Some 76,000 American and Philippine troops had become POWs by April 1943, and were marched 55 miles to the city of San Fernando for internment. Only 55,000 men managed to reach their destination; the rest died on the march due to exhaustion, exposure and hunger, or were killed by their Japanese captors. (NARA)

hands of a new French government acceptable to Germany. This new government, with its capital at Vichy, though nominally independent, was in fact under the thumb of the Germans. If the Vichy government were to displease them at any time, the Germans could quickly gobble up the unoccupied portion of France.

With the actual arrival of Allied troops in French North Africa, Allied planners were unsure of Vichy's sympathies under the new circumstances. The Allies hoped that the French forces in North Africa would join the Allied cause, but such an alliance had been tried before, leaving behind a legacy of bitterness. When the Franco-German armistice was announced in June 1940, the Royal Navy had acted quickly to ensure that the French Fleet would not join the Axis forces. The French Fleet was given an ultimatum: join the British, send the Fleet to the West Indies for the duration, or scuttle themselves. When the French Admiral refused, the British opened fire and sank virtually the entire fleet at Mers-el-Kebir Naval Station near Oran.

Once again desiring French co-operation, the Allies decided on a more diplomatic course in dealing with the French forces in North Africa. Days before the actual invasion, plans were made to contact by radio key French officers in Morocco who were thought to be sympathetic to the Allied cause and to convince them to throw in with the Allied cause, or at the least not oppose the landings. As the invasion was about to begin, the Allies decided to send several officers to convey this message personally. All of the officers chosen for the task were American; British participation would be purposely downplayed.

Colonel William Hale Wilbur, assigned to the Western Task Force under the command of General Patton, was one of the emissaries sent to treat with French officials in Morocco. A combat veteran of WWI, he seemed a logical choice, particularly because he had attended the Ecole Superieur de Guerre as a classmate of General Charles de Gaulle.

Col. Wilbur, charged by Gen. Patton to contact Admiral Francois Michelier, the Vichy commander of French naval forces at Casablanca, set off equipped with a jeep, a radio, a white flag, and a letter from Gen. Patton. Col. Wilbur came ashore with the first wave of assault troops at Fedala, about 12 miles north of Casablanca, and immediately things began to go wrong. Col. Wilbur's landing craft came under French machine gun fire, and once ashore Col. Wilbur found that his jeep was no longer operable. Commandeering a new vehicle, Col. Wilbur began his drive toward Casablanca in search of Adm. Michelier.

When he reached French Army positions under a flag of truce, he was escorted to the headquarters of the Casablanca Division where he was told by General Raymond Desre, that his intermediate contact, division commander Major-General E. Bethouart (an officer whom the Americans had contacted prior to the invasion), had been placed under arrest for treason. Col. Wilbur told Gen. Desre of Gen. Patton's letter, but

At the time of the Moroccan landings, Colonel William Wilbur (shown here as a brigadier-general) was sent by Gen. Patton to deliver a sensitive letter to a Vichy French commander at Oran. Arriving at French headquarters, Col. Wilbur could not get the French even to take the letter, never mind act upon it. (NARA)

At all three TORCH landing sites there had been French resistance, some lethargic and some intense. Once ashore, the Allies, who thought of themselves as liberators, had a difficult time finding French officials who had the authority to halt hostilities. Finally, Vichy Admiral J. F. Darlan was able to work out an armistice, but was himself assassinated on Christmas Eve 1942. (NARA)

the French commander, worried about the possible complications of collaboration with the Americans, refused to take the letter. In frustration, Col. Wilbur demanded that Gen. Desre take the letter, leaving it on the desk as he walked out of the French headquarters. As Col. Wilbur walked back to his car, a French officer approached him and offered to escort the Colonel to Adm. Michelier's headquarters. Col. Wilbur's arrival turned out to be anti-climactic, however; the French Admiral refused to see him. Recognizing that he could do no more, Col. Wilbur returned to the American positions at Fedala.

Safely back at Fedala, the Colonel noticed that most of the resistance around the beaches had ended with the exception of one battery of guns on the Cap de Fedala that was firing on the American fleet offshore. Sizing up the situation around the battery, Col. Wilbur, as the senior officer present, organized a scratch force consisting of four Stuart tanks from the 765th Tank Battalion and an infantry company to assault the French guns. Hopping aboard the lead tank, Col. Wilbur ordered the infantry to fan out while the tanks ploughed through the barbed wire that surrounded the battery. Advancing behind the M3s but still under heavy machine gun fire, the infantry captured the fire control bunker and then surprised and captured the battery. Col. Wilbur was awarded the Medal of Honor for conduct that was "voluntary and exemplary in its coolness and daring."

During the war Col. Wilbur rose to the rank of brigadier-general and was awarded the Silver Star, Bronze Star, two Legions of Merit, and the Combat Infantry Badge. He was also named a Knight Commander of the Order of Saint Maurice. Following his retirement from the Army in 1947, he wrote several books, including *The Making of George Washington* and *Freedom Must Not Perish*. He became a member of the Chicago Crime Commission and served as Warden of Cook County Jail before his death in 1979 at age 91.

Private Nicholas Minue

After the immediate gains of the TORCH invasion were consolidated, the focus of the Allied military effort in North Africa shifted from Morocco and Algeria to Axis-held Tunisia. By the end of 1942, the Axis forces that had earlier threatened Egypt had been pushed westward across Libya and the Allies were poised to wrest the entire North African coastline from them. Tunisia, however, proved a tough nut to crack and the deficiencies of the Allied armies and their command structure would become apparent as the Allied attack bogged down at the end of November and December. By the spring of 1943, American efforts were focused on driving through Axis defense lines and taking the Tunisian towns of Bizerte and Mateur, thereby cutting off Axis supply routes from Italy.

The 6th Armored Infantry of the US 1st Armored Division had been assigned the task of attacking enemy defensive positions in the Tine River valley, rough hilly country with rocky slopes, scrubby undergrowth, and steep cliffs. In the ranks of the 6th Infantry was Private Nicholas Minue, an unlikely hero. After 16 years of service in the Army (he had given up his sergeant's stripes to join a combat unit) the 44-year-old private from New Jersey was about to enter combat for the first time.

As the time for the attack approached, everyone knew that the enemy held all the high ground (the hills averaged 500 to 1,000 feet in height) and had had plenty of time to prepare a defense-in-depth of some 15 to 20 miles. The whole area was nicknamed the "Mouse Trap"; it was easy to get into but difficult to get out of. As an eye-witness put it, "the enemy on his hill positions was constantly looking right down your throat."

Claimed by both the Polish and Ukranian communities, Pvt. Nicholas Minue is shown wearing the enlisted pattern overcoat with his class A uniform. Barely visible on Minue's overseas cap is the enameled unit crest from the 6th Infantry Regiment. The unit went on to fight at Salerno, Anzio, up the Italian peninsula to Rome, and into northern Italy. (NARA)

By April 28, the 6th Armored Infantry Regiment had already seen some rather stiff fighting in its efforts to open the Tine River valley for the advance of the tank column. Pvt. Minue and the rest of A Company were assigned the task of assaulting Hill 299, a roughly horseshoe-shaped position held by German infantry, protected by barbed wire entanglements, mines, and four German machine gun positions. At 1600 hrs the Battalion began its assault on Hill 299. Almost immediately the attack encountered stiff enemy resistance and A Company became pinned down by flanking fire from an entrenched German machine gun. Pvt. Minue, with his company under fire, took matters into his own hands. He fixed bayonet to rifle, left cover, and charged one of the dug-in machine gun positions, manned by ten Germans. Despite heavy fire, Pvt. Minue managed to dispatch all the defenders with rifle fire and cold steel. Immediately another machine gun, this one from the enemy's second line, opened up on him and he rushed forward routing further enemy infantry from their foxholes. Pvt. Minue was fatally wounded in this second attack, yet his heroic example caused the men of A Company to move on and take the rest of the enemy positions on Hill 299. During the course of this attack, the Battalion took such heavy casualties that when they were relieved the next day, they had only 80 effectives.

Pvt. Minue is one of the few Medal of Honor recipients buried overseas, in the US Military Cemetery in Tunisia. Today his exploits are chiefly commemorated by an elementary school in Carteret, New Jersey, named in memory of his valiant sacrifice.

Gen. George S. Patton was the commander of the Western Task Force, the American contingent in the Allied invasion of Northwest Africa. Gen. Patton divided his time between combat and frustrating diplomacy with the French. Under his leadership, the untried American Army was worked into a powerful weapon the Germans in Tunisia would come to respect. (NARA)

Private Joe Martinez is pictured in the Army standard early wartime class A uniform, consisting of an olive-drab wool four-pocket tunic with branch of service insignia disks on the upper portion of the collar, white shirt, and black tie. The cap is the enlisted version of the service dress cap in dark olive-drab wool, displaying a disk with the national eagle in brass. (NARA)

Private Joe P. Martinez

While the Japanese (in the Battles of the Coral Sea and Midway) attempted to knock out the American aircraft carriers missed at Pearl Harbor, the Japanese High Command decided upon a feint to the Aleutians. Admiral Boshiro Hosagaya was tasked with the dual mission of seizing the islands of Kiska and Attu and the destruction of American forces at the base of Dutch Harbor.

Japanese naval landing forces took Kiska and Attu early in June 1942, and began construction of airfields on both of them. The Japanese did not have any real capability of successfully invading North America by way of the Aleutians, however. The islands were of small importance to American strategic plans, but they had great psychological value to the American people as the only territory held by the Japanese in the Western Hemisphere. As a result, the American High Command decided to eliminate these Japanese bases at the earliest possible date.

In March 1943, Admiral Thomas C. Kinkaid, the American commander in the Northern Pacific, established a naval blockade of both Kiska and Attu as an opening move to weaken the Japanese garrison prior to invasion. American plans called for an invasion of Attu, which was thought by Allied intelligence to have a garrison of only 500 men. In reality, there were over 1,000 Japanese troops on Attu and an additional 4,000 on Kiska. Accordingly, Adm. Kinkaid went forward with preparations for Operation SANDCRAB, gathering a task force of three battleships, one escort carrier, and seven destroyers to provide support for the ground assault of Attu, an assault to be undertaken by the 7th Infantry Division.

The island of Attu is approximately 35 miles long by 15 miles wide with a steep set of central ridges that run like a spine down the center of the island and slope toward the beaches. Most of the valleys are treeless and provide little or no cover for an attacking force. In addition, the island is covered with muskeg: a type of soggy bog composed of dead plants, peat, and other decomposed muck, a terrain feature not favoring an attacker.

The main landings on Attu began on May 11, 1943. That day, Private Joe Martinez, a member of K Company, 32nd Infantry, came ashore at "Red" Beach at Holtz Bay, north of the Japanese main base at Chichagof Harbor. Pvt. Martinez, a 22-year-old draftee from Colorado, was seeing his first action in the cold and mist of the far north. A combination of bad weather, difficult terrain, and unexpectedly stiff Japanese resistance had slowed the American advance to a crawl, but by May 24, American superior numbers and fire power began taking their toll on the Japanese defenders. K Company cleared the Chichagof Pass and took a Japanese position on a steep ridge called the "Bahai", or Fish Hook.

As the Americans advanced, they encountered Japanese defenders in small foxholes in front of the main position. Pvt. Martinez was his platoon's Browning automatic rifle gunner, and his job was to provide fire support to cover the advance. Initially, the Japanese defense of Chichagof was weak and the Americans steadily drove back the defenders toward their main positions until reaching the Fish Hook, where the defense stiffened. Pvt. Martinez, according to one of his comrades, "got mad" and jumped up from his cover and began running from one Japanese position to another spraying the defenders with bullets. When he had expended his BAR ammunition, he picked up an M1 Garand rifle and continued his one-man assault of the Japanese. His sergeant, Earl Marks, described Pvt. Martinez "as a Wildman... and a tornado".

The Americans, inspired by Pvt. Martinez' bravery, advanced to the base of the Japanese position on the Fish Hook. By this time, the company was down to 18 riflemen and 6 BAR gunners. Temperatures were dropping and the Japanese defenders were firmly entrenched on a ridge that sloped up 45 degrees from its base to the firing positions on the crest. As K Company neared the top of a pass overlooking the Japanese position, Pvt. Martinez again jumped up from his position and, standing on a rock ledge in full view of the Japanese, began to fire into the Japanese trench with his BAR, firing round after round into the Japanese infantry, eventually expending three clips of ammunition. Suddenly, a hand grenade exploded and Pvt. Martinez fell, mortally wounded.

The next morning, American forces found that the Japanese had pulled out under the cover of darkness, leaving 40 Japanese dead in two trenches in front of the position attacked by Pvt. Martinez.

This photograph, from a wartime edition of *YANK* magazine, shows a pair of US soldiers after the fall of Attu in the Aleutians. They hold captured Japanese souvenirs, a small infantry standard, and a bottle of sake. The background shows the steep open terrain around the Chichagof pass. (NARA)

Pvt. Martinez lies buried in his hometown of Ault, Colorado, and a statue of him stands on the lawn of the Colorado State Capitol. A Disabled American Veterans chapter and an American Legion post are named in his honor.

Corporal Charles E. "Commando" Kelly

At the end of May 1943, the Allied push across Tunisia succeeded in sealing off the remaining Axis troops in North Africa in the Cap Bon Peninsula, forcing their surrender. At Casablanca in January 1943, President Franklin D. Roosevelt and Prime Minister Winston Churchill agreed that Sicily would be the next invasion target, with the threefold objective of clearing the central Mediterranean for Allied shipping, tying down Axis troops which might otherwise be sent as reinforcements to Russia, and eliminating Italy as an Axis power. The invasion, Operation HUSKY, was launched on July 10, 1943, with eight Allied divisions, ending 38 days later with the surrender of the last Axis resistance. Within a month of the Axis defeat in Sicily, the British landed at Reggio on the toe of Italy and at Taranto on the heel, and six days later the American Operation AVALANCHE, the invasion of mainland Italy, was launched at Salerno, southeast of Naples.

Part of this invasion force was the American 36th Infantry Division, a National Guard division made up of soldiers drawn mostly from Texas and Oklahoma. An inexperienced formation, fresh from advanced training in North Africa, they were anxious to make their mark in combat. The "T-Patchers" of the 36th Division came ashore at Salerno on September 9, 1943, against light German resistance and immediately moved inland. By the end of the first day, the boys of the 36th established a lodgment area five miles from the beachhead.

On September 13, the 3rd Battalion of the 36th Division's 143rd Regiment was ordered to attack a German hilltop position northwest of the village of Altavilla. In this action, the Battalion's L Company was to act as a reserve. Although in reserve, L Company's Charles E. Kelly's war began that day. Corporal Kelly, a native of Pittsburgh, Pennsylvania, was born in 1920 and had grown up in a tough North side neighborhood, famous for its junkyards and barns converted into houses for the poor. Kelly, one of nine brothers, was forced to leave school at age 14 to take a job as a house painter. From this impoverished background, Army life seemed almost luxurious and Kelly took to it with gusto. Always the first to volunteer for action, Corp. Kelly soon established a reputation for reckless aggressiveness.

It was not surprising, therefore, when Corp. Kelly volunteered to reconnoiter the German position that the Battalion had been ordered to attack. Returning with his report of the enemy's strength, Kelly soon went off to conduct a second reconnaissance of the enemy positions west of the town of Altavilla. With him he took his BAR and two infantrymen to act as assistants, carrying extra ammunition for the BAR and providing covering fire for Corp. Kelly whenever he moved to a new position. As the trio of Americans moved out of Altavilla, they came under heavy fire from a hidden German machine gun position. Corp. Kelly hurriedly deployed the BAR and with highly accurate fire, silenced the German gun. On his return, Corp. Kelly reported that the Germans were in great strength around Hill 424 and that they were planning a counterattack against the Americans in the village. Since Corp. Kelly had exhausted the ammunition for his BAR, he requested permission to go into Altavilla to obtain more ammunition. Given permission, Corp. Kelly was also ordered to set up an ammunition supply line to get much needed matériel to the front line troops outside Altavilla.

Soon after Corp. Kelly left, the Germans began their attack with a heavy barrage of artillery and mortar fire on the American positions around the village. Arriving on the scene, he found the house commandeered as a supply dump under fierce German attack. Corp. Kelly entered the house and concealed himself on an upper floor to get a good view, then began shooting back at the enemy. The German attack was intense, hitting the Americans from three sides with a combined force of infantry and armor. Soon the dozen or so men in the supply dump were cut off and Altavilla was isolated from the rest of the regiment. As darkness fell, the German attacks slackened in their frequency, yet the Germans continued to infiltrate the village through the night. Corp. Kelly and the rest of the beleaguered Americans in the house managed to hold out, but only just.

In the morning, the Germans again attacked the supply dump, and Corp. Kelly once again occupied his key position at the upstairs window and renewed his heroic defense. He kept a continuous fire on the advancing Germans until his BAR locked-up from overheating. Throwing the useless weapon onto a nearby bed, he snatched up another weapon and continued to fire at the enemy, heedless of the fact that the red hot barrel of his BAR had ignited the bedclothes. During the height of the German attack, with the room filling with smoke from the burning bed, Corp. Kelly could see from his vantage point that German infantry were sneaking closer to the house, using a ditch as cover. Without grenades, he scanned the room for something to counter this threat. He spotted a batch of 60mm mortar shells on the floor. He armed them, and then hurled them at the enemy, killing five and stopping the advance.

Enemy attacks continued throughout the rest of the day, but during a lull in the fighting Corp. Kelly abandoned his burnt-out position on the upper floor to see what was happening in the rest of the building. Going down to the kitchen, he found a group of GIs cooking spaghetti and drinking bottles of champagne. Surprised at first, he grabbed one of the bottles of champagne for himself and went back to the defense of the house.

The defenders received an order to pull out of the position. True to form, Corp. Kelly stayed to the last, firing a bazooka at enemy snipers in a nearby building. When he ran out of rockets for his bazooka, he left the house to take charge of a 37mm anti-tank gun that had been abandoned in front of the house. Here his adventure nearly came to an end; he fired the first shot in a hurry without checking the

In this photo from a later war bond drive, recently promoted Sergeant Kelly is wearing the 1942 pattern of the Army enlisted service dress jacket with a light olive-drab wool shirt and khaki tie. The decorations above the left breast pocket are the ribbon for the Medal of Honor and the European campaign ribbon. Note the fancy "zigzag" stitching on Sgt. Kelly's chevrons. (NARA)

This group of infantrymen is typical of American combat troops in the Italian campaign. The figure in the right foreground wears cotton coveralls in place of the more usual woolen trousers, shirt, and Parsons jacket worn by the others. (NARA)

angle of the barrel and the round crashed into the stone wall in front of the muzzle, showering him with stone fragments and wounding him slightly. Luckily, the round he'd fired had been a solid, armor-piercing round, not a high-explosive round, whose detonation at such close range would have killed him outright. Dazed from the shot, Corp. Kelly adjusted the sights and managed to fire over the wall at the advancing Germans. With enemy shots zipping around him, he at last withdrew from his position and made his way back to his unit under cover of darkness. It was for this continuous action that Kelly was awarded the Medal of Honor.

Following the fight at Altavilla, Corp. Kelly continued to serve in the 143rd, seeing action at the Battle of San Pietro and again at the crossing of the Rapido River, in addition to numerous smaller engagements. Returning to America on a war bond drive, he was the focus of a mass of attention from the media because he was one of the early recipients of the Medal of Honor for ground combat in Europe.

Like many war heroes, Corp. Kelly was an ideal combat soldier yet found peacetime difficult. His life following World War II was marked by personal tragedy and failed business ventures. Charles "Commando" Kelly, the man once dubbed the bravest man in America, died virtually forgotten in a Veterans' Administration hospital in 1984.

Major Matt Urban

Unlike the majority of Medal of Honor recipients, Capt. Urban was awarded the medal, not for one act of bravery, but a series of actions that occurred from June 14 to September 3, 1944, in the immediate aftermath of the Normandy invasion.

Capt. Urban commanded F Company, 2nd Battalion, 60th Infantry Regiment of the 9th Infantry Division. The 9th, "Old Reliables", came ashore on Utah Beach on D+4, June 10, 1944, and went into action westward of the beachhead on the Merderet River near the village of Ste Colombe. Four days later, on June 14, Capt. Urban's company moved into the French village of Renouf. As the 2nd Battalion began its advance, Capt. Urban's F Company moved toward the village and came under attack from a pair of German tanks which opened fire on his men with their main guns as well as machine guns. As his men scattered to seek cover, Capt. Urban grabbed a bazooka and worked his way to within 45yds of the enemy. Using the cover provided by a hedgerow, he accompanied one soldier carrying ammunition and stalked the deadly tanks.

Carefully putting himself into position, Capt. Urban destroyed first one German vehicle and then the other with his bazooka. Inspired by the bravery of their commanding officer, Company F re-formed and with a cheer pushed into Renouf, rooting out the enemy from their defensive positions.

Later that same day, as Company F continued its attack toward the town of Orglandes, Capt. Urban was wounded in the leg by fire from a German 37mm anti-tank gun. Although the calf of his left leg was severely injured, he refused to be evacuated and continued to direct the men of his company from a litter carried by two of his soldiers. Placing his troops into defensive positions, Capt. Urban sat down to wait until morning when the American attack could be renewed. As morning broke, the wounded Captain led his company in another attack south of the town of Orglandes, where he was wounded a second time. At last, weakened from loss of blood, Capt. Urban permitted himself to be evacuated to an aid station and from there to a military hospital in the south of England.

In July, during his recovery in England, Capt. Urban learned the 60th had been badly cut up in the fighting in the hedgerow country of Normandy and that the Battalion Commander had been wounded and sent to the United States. Realizing the need for experienced officers in the fighting across the Channel, Capt. Urban was unwilling just to sit while his men were being killed. He checked himself out of the hospital, obtained passage aboard a ship bound for Normandy, and made his way back to the front near St. Lo where his company had been fighting. When Capt. Urban arrived at 2nd Battalion headquarters on July 25, 1944, he discovered that his company had already begun a fresh attack. Limping along with a stick he used as a cane in one hand and a gun in the other hand, Capt. Urban managed to rejoin his men at a critical juncture in the fighting.

Lieutenant-Colonel Matt Urban received the Medal of Honor for his exploits in the days following the Normandy invasion in 1944. The award, however, was not made until 1980, due to a mix-up in paper work. With the belated award of the Medal of Honor, Matt Urban joined Audie Murphy to be counted as one of the two most decorated US soldiers of World War II. (Home of Heroes)

A sergeant later said: "One of the craziest officers suddenly appeared before us, yelling like a madman and waving a gun in his hand… He got us on our feet, though, gave us our confidence back and saved our lives."

Company F was pinned down by heavy enemy fire and a group of three Sherman tanks from the 746th Armored Battalion had been called in for support. When Capt. Urban arrived on the scene, he found that two of the US tanks had already been knocked-out and the third was out of action due to crew casualties. Capt. Urban quickly found a lieutenant and a sergeant from the 746th and together they scurried toward the undamaged tank. Under thick German machine gun fire, first the lieutenant and then the sergeant were killed before either could reach the tank. Thinking that his time was about to run out, Capt. Urban nevertheless hobbled forward and managed to reach the tank and squeeze into the turret despite the bullets ricocheting all around him. Finding the driver still inside, Capt. Urban gave the order to advance while he manned the vehicle's .50-cal. machine gun and blasted the enemy strong point that held up the advance. Faced with this example of impetuous leadership, troops from the 2nd Battalion leaped up from their foxholes and successfully stormed the enemy position.

What followed in the next few days was a spectacular freewheeling advance by American troops as they at last began to break-out of the hedgerow country and enter an area more suited to mobile warfare. General Omar Bradley, commander of the newly formed 12th US Army Group, was determined that the American forces in France would destroy the German 7th Army before they could cross the Seine River and erect a new defensive line.

During a last-ditch German effort to disrupt the American advance at Mortain, Capt. Urban was again wounded, earning him his fifth Purple Heart. In spite of shell fragments lodged in his chest, he refused evacuation and stayed with the company to continue its advance. Promoted major on the spot on August 6, 1944, Urban assumed command of the 2nd Battalion whose previous commander had been killed in a counterattack at Mortain. Wounded again on August 15, Maj. Urban continued commanding the Battalion, pushing the men to the very border of Belgium by the beginning of September. During that advance, on the second day of September 1944, the war came to an end for Maj. Urban when he was wounded in the throat as his troops forced a crossing of the Meuse River.

Maj. Urban was medically discharged from the US Army in 1946 after extensive surgery and speech therapy which left

Soldiers of the 60th Infantry walk alongside a Sherman tank during an advance. The Sherman shows two examples of field modifications made to suit the changing nature of the war. Appliqué armor has been applied to both the turret and side hull and a hedge cutter constructed from German beach obstacles has been attached to the front. (NARA)

him with a raspy voice. He later moved to the town of Holland, Michigan, where he was active in organizing sports for young people. It was not until 1978, when a war buddy inquired of the Army why Maj. Urban had not received the Medal of Honor, that a board of inquiry was formed to look into the matter. Apparently, the letter of recommendation had never reached the proper authorities! On July 19, 1980, after a delay of 35 years, Lieutenant-Colonel Matt Urban was presented the Medal of Honor by President Jimmy Carter. One of America's most decorated soldiers, Col. Urban died at the age of 75 in 1995 from a collapsed lung, the complication from a war wound. "The Ghost," a nickname given to him by the Germans because he kept coming back to fight despite wounds, is buried in Arlington National Cemetery.

Private Harold A. Garman

Army medics, like their Navy corpsmen counterparts in the Pacific, played a heroic and dangerous part on the battlefields of World War II. Among this gallant group was 26-year-old Harold Garman of Fairfield, Illinois, a medic attached to the 5th Medical Battalion of the 5th Infantry Division when it landed in France on July 9, 1944. The division immediately moved to the front to relieve the 1st Infantry Division and became involved in Operation COBRA, General Omar Bradley's plan to break out from the Normandy bridgehead. The attack was such a great success that it opened the way for a breakneck advance across France.

In both the North African and European theaters of operations, medics wore special insignia into action to distinguish them as non-combatants. Here Private Harold Garman wears the M1 steel helmet in olive-drab, painted with the distinctive white circle and red cross. (NARA)

As an infantry division, the 5th was hard put to keep pace with the mechanized units of the American Army in the breakout. In order to do so, all non-essential equipment was left behind; even field kitchens were stripped of their trucks to transport troops. As a result, everyone lived on K-rations. To keep up with the advance across France, men would catch rides atop armored vehicles – 10 men on a Sherman tank and 12 on an M10 tank destroyer – while others rode packed into jeeps or any other vehicle that they could find.

As the 5th moved across France, all eyes were on the next major natural barrier, the Seine River. Everyone wondered if the German defense of the river could stem the tide of advance or if the Germans would break under the American assault. Upon reaching the Seine, the 10th Regimental Combat Team (RCT), to which Pvt. Garman was attached, was to assault the town of Montereau, 70 miles south of Paris, and to seize a bridgehead across the Seine River.

On August 25, 1944, a river crossing was led by two battalions of the 10th RCT who paddled themselves across in small assault boats. Under cover of darkness and a barrage provided by the regimental artillery, the first wave of troops began their crossing at 2105 hrs. Encountering only weak opposition, the First and then the Second Battalion of the 10th RCT crossed the Seine and seized the high ground on the opposite shore. They hurriedly set up defensive positions to await the inevitable German counterattack.

The Germans struck with the early morning fog and pounded the American defenders. As casualties mounted, the 70 assault boats were now pressed into service to bring the wounded back to the evacuation centers on the far bank. As the boats neared the middle of the river, mortar and machine gun fire cut into one of them, killing some of the occupants and causing the others to dive into the water. Pvt. Garman, who had been assigned as a litter bearer, was watching from shore when he noticed that one of the occupants of the assault boat was too badly wounded to swim. He immediately jumped into the water and swam toward the stricken craft. As the German fire churned the water around him, Pvt. Garman reached the boat and found not one but three wounded men clinging to the far side of the boat for protection. Unable to swim ashore with three wounded men, he began towing the boat to shore. Despite heavy fire, he managed to bring the three wounded men to the safety of the south bank amid the cheers of his fellow soldiers. Galvanized by his bravery, troops on the southern shore of the Seine pushed additional boats into the water and rowed to the northern shore, some to join the fight and others to aid in the rescue efforts.

By the end of that day, the 5th Division had successfully established, and held, three separate bridgeheads over the Seine, virtually ensuring that the Germans would be unable to defend the city of Paris. Gen. Patton presented the Medal of Honor in the field to Pvt. Garman, who continued serving with the 5th Division through the rest of the French Campaign, the Battle of the Bulge, and the push into southern Germany.

Sergeant Oscar G. Johnson

By the summer of 1944, the invasion of France was successful but the future of the Italian campaign was in doubt. The Germans had promptly occupied Italy when Mussolini was deposed in July 1943. The new Italian government had seemed to be wavering in its loyalty to the Axis, and after hard fighting at the Salerno beachhead, the Germans slowly retreated to the powerful fortifications of the Gustav line, protecting Rome. However, the city fell on June 4, 1944, and the Allies proceeded rapidly up the peninsula, reaching the Gothic Line north of Florence at the end of August. Sensing an opportunity to crack Germany's southern defenses and arrive in central Europe before the Red Army, Churchill pressed the Allied commanders to redouble their efforts and pushed for an offensive to break the Gothic Line. This was the origin of Operation OLIVE.

It began with an attack by the British 8th Army along a 17-mile front near the coastal town of Pesaro on the Adriatic. Allied commanders hoped that this attack would force the Germans to commit their reserves and allow the Americans to punch through the Gothic line defenses at Il Giogo Pass.

The Allied attack was to be along a 60-mile front, with the center being held by the US II Corps, made up of the 34th, 85th, 88th, and 91st Infantry Divisions. The 363rd Infantry Regiment, 91st "Powder River" Infantry Division, was to be one of the units that would bear the brunt of the effort in the upcoming attack. Private First Class Oscar G. Johnson, a native of Foster City, Michigan, waited anxiously for the word to move out, as did every one of his buddies in the 363rd Regiment's B Company.

The 91st Division began its assault on the German defenses on September 12, 1944, and although involved in a series of small unit actions, the Americans could not use their numerical superiority to advantage. The terrain was familiar to these experienced soldiers: steep rocky ridges divided by deep narrow valleys and flanked by rugged mountains that channeled all movement into the defenders' fields of fire.

The 363rd, on the extreme left flank of the 91st Division, assaulted the Monticelli ridge, which overlooked the primary American objective, Il Giogo Pass. Moving from one scrap of cover to the next, B Company clawed its way up the slope under heavy German machine gun and mortar fire. By the evening of the 14th, the lead platoons were pinned down by accurate fire from a concealed strong point.

Finally, at dawn the German position was found by an American reconnaissance patrol and B Company called down an artillery strike. Under the cover of the barrage, the company fixed bayonets and charged the German defenders to take Monticelli Ridge. Pfc. Johnson and his fellow mortar men soon used up their supply of ammunition and were temporarily converted into riflemen. Leading a scratch squad of seven men, Pfc. Johnson was in the most advanced position, some 50yds beyond the left flank of the company. The full fury of a German counterattack descended upon Johnson and his small band. The German attacks lasted throughout the day of the 16th and by mid-afternoon all of the defenders on the left flank except for Johnson had either been killed or seriously wounded. Undaunted, Pfc. Johnson continued to hold his position, forced to scramble under enemy fire to gather up weapons and ammunition from the dead and wounded lying around him in a grim effort to hold his position at all costs.

The Germans moved close enough to throw grenades into Johnson's small trench. That night they launched their heaviest counterattack to date. Standing up under the hail of fire, Pfc. Johnson beat back the enemy attack with a barrage of grenades and rifle fire. Such was the fury of his defense that on the morning of the 17th, 25 German paratroopers surrendered to him. Finally, with the German pressure slackening, the company spared two soldiers to reinforce Pfc. Johnson. However, before they could reach him, both men were wounded by German artillery. In one final act of desperate bravery, Pfc.

Sergeant Oscar Johnson has just been awarded the Medal of Honor by Gen. Mark Clark (center) and is congratulated by a colonel who undoubtedly has just taken part in the award ceremony. It was an affectation of Gen. Clark's troops to adopt a blue scarf for dress occasions, but Sgt. Johnson has removed his, possibly to emphasize the medal at his throat. (NARA)

Johnson dashed to where the two badly wounded men were lying and gave covering fire while a medic applied first aid. Then he and the medic dragged the men to safety.

When relief finally arrived that night, there were only 50 fit men remaining in the entire company, with all officers and NCOs dead or wounded. In their desperate defense, Pfc. Johnson and the men of B Company had lived up to the unit motto "ILLIGITMUS NON CARBORUNDUM" – "Don't let the bastards grind you down".

Despite the casualties suffered by B Company, the attack against the Gothic line had been a success with the American 5th Army breaching the German defenses along a seven-mile front. The coming of winter delayed capture of the Gothic Line until spring 1945. Soon after, on May 2, 1945, German forces in Italy finally surrendered, only days before the surrender of Germany itself.

Promoted due to the heavy loss of officers and NCOs in his company, now Sergeant Johnson was awarded the Medal of Honor by General Mark Clark in Trieste in April of 1945, and remained with the 363rd until war's end. He returned to Michigan and served in the Michigan National Guard until April 1964 when he retired with the rank of Chief Warrant Officer. He died in 1999.

Private First Class Joe E. Mann

By September 1944, an early victory over Germany seemed imminent. The Red Army was moving like a juggernaut toward the German border from the east. The combined Allied bombing campaign had wrought havoc on the German armed forces, people, industry, and communications network. In the west, three major Allied armies were poised on the German border from the Netherlands south to Switzerland.

Although the pre-Normandy invasion plans called for a thrust into the industrial Ruhr Valley, Field Marshal Bernard Montgomery now pushed for a strong northern drive by his 21st Army from the Netherlands across the Rhine all the way to Berlin. Generals Bradley and Patton proposed their own all-out thrust across the Rhine in the area of Wiesbaden and Mannheim.

Gen. Eisenhower, who had taken over command of all Allied forces in Europe on September 1, 1944, recognized that supply and logistics problems exacerbated by the rapid advance across France could support only one offensive into Germany. Gen. Eisenhower, therefore, decided to gamble on Montgomery's northern thrust, but limited the goal to the seizure of a bridgehead over the Rhine from which future attacks into Germany could be mounted when the supply situation was improved.

The plan, Operation MARKET, was to lay down an "airborne carpet" in front of an advancing armored thrust by the British Second Army, called Operation GARDEN. MARKET committed the

This is the only known photograph of Private First Class Joe Mann. Of interest is the large circular patch, whose detail has been obliterated by the censor, on the left hand side of the private's overseas cap. This patch showed a glider and parachute on a large machine embroidered circle, the distinctive badge of the American parachute infantry. (NARA)

1st Airborne Army, composed of American, British, and Polish components, to take and hold bridges at Eindhoven, Nijmegen, and Arnhem, allowing the British armor to advance swiftly to consolidate their hold on the Rhine crossing at Arnhem.

The American 101st Airborne Division would land in the southernmost drop zone, near the Dutch border town of Eindhoven. The Division's 502nd Parachute Infantry Regiment, veterans of the Normandy invasion, were to take the road bridge at Dommel, secure the town of Saint Oendenrode, defend drop zones B and C for glider landings, and then seize a crossing over the Wilhelmina Canal.

The 101st's landings on September 17, 1944, went according to plan, with most of the men landing close together. Immediately, the 502nd set out on their ambitious objectives, seizing both the town of Saint Oendenrode and the Dommel Bridge with great rapidity. As they advanced on the Wilhelmina Canal, they were hit by stubborn German resistance. The next day, Company H, under a Lieutenant named Wierzbowski, was to attempt to take a concrete road bridge over the canal near the town of Best.

Moving out with H Company's advance platoon was Private Joe Mann, a 22-year-old from Washington State, who had been with the 101st since completing basic training in 1943. Under constant harassing fire, Lt. Wierzbowski led his 15-man patrol toward Best and got them into position within 200yds of the bridge, but found it too heavily defended to be taken by such a small force. The deadlock was resolved when the Germans, perhaps fearing that the lone patrol was an advance element of a larger force, destroyed the bridge and withdrew.

Stunned by the sudden destruction of their objective, Lt. Wierzbowski spotted a German 88mm gun position nearby and ordered Privates Mann and Hoyle to destroy the gun. With Mann acting as the lead scout and Hoyle carrying a bazooka, the two "Screaming Eagles" crept to within range of the German gun. Crossing his fingers for luck, Private Hoyle let fly with the bazooka and knocked out the 88mm with his first shot. The German support crew spotted the two Americans and a firefight ensued. Engaging them with his rifle, Pfc. Mann picked off the German crew one by one, in spite of receiving several minor wounds in the process.

As the afternoon wore on, Lt. Wierzbowski became aware that he and his dwindling patrol were cut off from the rest of H Company. The situation was made even worse by a sudden German counter-attack. Several of the defenders were wounded, including Pfc. Mann, who was hit in both arms and incapacitated. For an unknown reason, the German commander halted the attack that would otherwise surely have ended in the destruction of Lt. Wierzbowski's small command. Digging in, the Americans resigned themselves to spending a miserable night holding on to their toehold in the town.

With the dawn the Germans renewed the attack. Almost immediately a grenade landed in the midst of the American defenders. Unable to use his arms, Pfc. Mann shouted "Grenade!" and threw himself on the "potato masher", saving his comrades at the cost of his own life. With all his men either killed or wounded, Lt. Wierzbowski had no choice but to surrender his battered patrol to the Germans.

The paratroopers' fortunes changed once more, when they were rescued by their returning comrades of the 502nd and the 101st who had gone on to secure the necessary bridges to support the British advance. Unfortunately, Operation MARKET-GARDEN ultimately turned into a costly failure when the British tank force was unable to reach Arnhem before the Germans counterattacked in strength.

Ideally, the paratrooper was to be able to defend himself immediately when his feet touched the ground, as shown in this training photograph. In actual combat, however, many found themselves barely able to gain their footing after landing, encumbered as they were with nearly 100lbs. of equipment. (NARA)

After the war, Pfc. Mann's Medal of Honor was given to his parents who later dedicated a memorial to him in Best, Holland. An open-air theater at the New Museum in Best is also dedicated to him.

Captain James M. Burt

With the failure of MARKET-GARDEN, Gen. Eisenhower reviewed his options for the invasion of Germany. Presented with a choice between the southern, Saar, corridor and the northern, Aachen, corridor, the Supreme Allied Commander chose the northern approach. The forces beginning the thrust were the British 21st Army Group on the northern flank, the US 6th Army Group on the southern flank, and the US 12th Army Group in the center. The 12th Army Group was composed of the 9th Army under General William H. Simpson, General George S. Patton's 3rd Army, and General Courtney Hodges' 1st Army, which included the 2nd Armored Division.

As the 1st Army began penetrating the Siegfried line, the German fortifications that ran along Germany's western border, Gen. Hodges decided to encircle and neutralize the historic city of Aachen because it posed a threat to the left flank of his VII Corps.

On October 1, 1944, the 1st Infantry Division isolated the city of Aachen from the south, while the XIX Corps accomplished the same from the north. Initially, XIX Corps' 30th Infantry Division began the encirclement by crossing the Wurm River and assaulting West Wall positions. On October 3, the infantry had established a bridgehead and called up the 2nd Armored Division to cross the Wurm to move into position for the attack.

With the 2nd Armored Division that day was Captain James M. Burt, in command of B Company of the 66th Armored Regiment. A native of Massachusetts, Capt. Burt had put himself through Norwich College with the help of academic and football scholarships and a part-time job. He joined the Reserve Officers' Training Corps while at Norwich, graduated with a degree in Chemistry, and took a job in the paper industry before entering the Army.

Capt. Burt's company was to support the infantry units of the 30th Division in an attack designed to complete the encirclement of the German garrison inside Aachen. During the initial infantry assaults into the city's northern suburb of Wurselen, the units of the 30th Division ran into heavy small arms and mortar fire that slowed their attack. At this point Capt. Burt halted his advance, dismounted from his tank, and ran forward to see how he could best deploy his tanks to aid the infantry. Returning to his tank despite heavy fire, the Captain calmly directed his tanks forward into positions from which they could direct raking fire into the enemy. With this timely assistance, the infantry was at last able to regain the initiative and began the advance again. Capt.

Captain James Burt is pictured in this official wartime photograph wearing service dress uniform, consisting of a dark olive-drab tunic and overseas cap, tan gabardine shirt and tie. The devices that are affixed to the lower portion of his lapels are brass rhomboid WWI tanks, symbols of the American armored forces. (NARA)

American infantry advance through a section of the Siegfried Line. The line was littered with a variety of obstacles to stop tank attacks, such as the "Dragon's teeth" to the right of the road and the pair of ramps each side of the road designed to force tanks to expose their lightly armored undersides. (NARA)

Burt, climbing back onto his tank, began to direct the assault from the tank's top deck behind the turret, and continued to advance until coming upon a group of German self-propelled guns. Still in his exposed position atop his tank, Capt. Burt was hit by shrapnel fragments but remained in contact with the enemy until artillery fire was called down on the German guns. Once again able to go forward, he carefully positioned his tanks to defend the ground gained by the day's combined arms action.

During the next week of action, Capt. Burt was never far from the action, leading his men from the front, and inspiring them to continue the advance against stiff enemy resistance. At one point, he drove his tank into the midst of an enemy position and called down accurate artillery fire on the position. Twice during this week, the tank in which he was riding was knocked out by enemy fire. Each time he found a new tank and pushed on, until the "Aachen Gap" was closed and the city encircled. For both his coolness under fire and his superb leadership, Capt. Burt was awarded the Medal of Honor for his week-long attack north of Aachen.

Following the war, he returned to his prewar occupation in the paper industry, where he eventually rose to Vice-President of Sales for a large paper company. Retiring after 20 years, James Burt became an associate professor of Mathematics and Physics at Franklin Pierce College in New Hampshire, and retired 11 years later at age 72. Capt. Burt lives quietly today in Wyomissing, Pennsylvania, interrupted only by engagements as an inspirational speaker around the country.

Lieutenant-Colonel George L. Mabry, Jr.

Landing at Utah Beach on June 6, 1944, and taking part in the rapid breakthrough from the bridgehead in Normandy, the 4th Infantry Division fought its way across Europe in four months. By November, they found themselves engaged in their bloodiest battle of the war: in the Hurtgen Forest in western Germany. Men plodded ahead in cold rain and snow amidst a forest of pine and fir trees 150ft high. The advance was slow but relentless, fought day-by-day, and often yard-by-yard against fierce resistance. Rifle company casualties were often as much as 250 percent of the original force. Gen. Patton called it an "epic of stark infantry combat".

In late November 1944, Lieutenant-Colonel George L. Mabry, Jr., then a captain, was in command of the 2nd Battalion, 8th Infantry. Capt. Mabry, who had been awarded the Silver Star for his D-Day exploits, found himself and his men in the middle of a minefield as they crossed the dunes on Utah beach on D-Day. Under fire, Capt. Mabry had to choose between returning to the beach or advancing against the enemy. He led a 25yd bayonet charge which brought him to a German foxhole that he took at bayonet point. He then assaulted a German pillbox which guarded one of the areas planned for break-out from the beach. Next, he pushed on to a bridge, outflanked the defenders, and dismantled demolition charges. Once clear of the bridge, he moved on to a link-up with 101st Airborne troops in Poupeville.

Mabry, born in rural South Carolina in 1917, had enrolled in the Reserve Officers' Training Corps when he entered college, and graduated as a Second Lieutenant in 1940. Assigned to the newly formed 4th Infantry Division at Fort Benning, Georgia, he trained in the US and England, and entered Fortress Europe in the second wave at Utah Beach on June 6, 1944. The Division went on across the Cotentin Peninsula to take Cherbourg, and then liberated Paris. After preventing the fall of Luxembourg City in the Battle of the Bulge, the Division breached the Siegfried Line and poured into the heartland of Germany. Capt. Mabry was always in the thick of action; so extraordinary had been his performance in combat that he received two battlefield promotions, advancing from captain to lieutenant-colonel in less than five months.

On November 20, Col. Mabry led his Battalion in the divisional advance into the Hurtgen Forest, where the Battalion's advance bogged down when it reached a minefield and came under heavy enemy fire. He went ahead alone and carefully marked a way through the minefield. As his men came up, Mabry continued to lead from the front, going ahead of his point men. Again the way was blocked, this time by booby-trapped double concertina wire. With the help of several scouts, Mabry

This wartime photograph of Lieutenant-Colonel George L. Mabry, Jr., has been retouched by an official censor. Oddly enough, most insignia have been left un-retouched, while the shirt, which bore no insignia, has been completely repainted, giving a somewhat cartoon-like effect. (NARA)

Col. Mabry is shown receiving his Medal of Honor from President Harry Truman in 1945, just after the war's end. In addition to the US's highest decoration, he had also received the Silver Star, the Bronze Star, the Combat Infantryman's Badge, and the Distinguished Service Order, the highest British decoration awarded to foreigners. (NARA)

disconnected the explosives and they cut a way through the wire.

Coming out of the wire, Col. Mabry saw three Germans in a foxhole just ahead. He ran over and captured them at bayonet point. After the prisoners had been turned over, he led an attack on three mutually supporting log bunkers. Dashing up to the first bunker and finding it empty, he was running for the second when nine Germans rushed him. He rifle butted the first man and bayoneted a second before his scouts arrived and assisted him in subduing the remainder.

Turning then to the third bunker, Col. Mabry led his men in the face of intense small arms fire up and into the bunker where they took six more Germans at bayonet point. Mabry then consolidated their gains before leading his men 300yds further, to high ground. There he established an excellent defensive position which threatened both enemy flanks and provided a firm foothold on the approaches to the Cologne Plain.

Col. Mabry remained in the Army after the war, rising to the rank of major-general. He served in the Canal Zone, Korea, and completed two tours in Vietnam, where he was Chief of Staff and Assistant Deputy Commanding General, U.S. Army Forces, Vietnam. Gen. Mabry was awarded the Silver Star, Bronze Star for Valor with Arrowhead and Oakleaf Cluster, Purple Heart, Presidential Unit Citation, British Distinguished Service Order, Belgian Fourragere, the Combat Infantry Badge, and five campaign medals. He was considered, until the belated award of the Medal of Honor to Lt. Col. Matt Urban, to be the second most decorated soldier of World War II, after Audie Murphy.

He retired from the Army in 1975 and died on June 13, 1990, at age 72. In 1990, the Noncommissioned Officers' Academy at Fort Jackson, South Carolina, was dedicated in his honor.

Technical Sergeant Robert E. Gerstung

Heroism was not limited to desperate battles like the Hurtgen Forest. The Allied advance across Europe was a slow, plodding, day-in and day-out effort against savage German resistance. Winter was the worst in 50 years, adding the miseries of extreme cold and driving snow to those of warfare. In mid-December 1944, the 79th Division found itself part of the 7th Army line in Alsace.

The 79th Division, like the 4th, had landed at Utah Beach and taken part in the liberation of Cherbourg, an action fitting for the "Cross of Lorraine" Division, which had acquired its nickname during the First World War. After Cherbourg, the division was shifted far to the south to hold the Seventh Army flank in Alsace. They participated in the battle of Hagenau in early December and by December 15 had reached the Lauter River at Schiebenhardt, where they became engaged in the systematic reduction of the Siegfried Line.

On December 19, 29-year-old Chicago native Technical Sergeant Robert E. Gerstung took his heavy machine gun squad to support an infantry assault against the German line near Berg, on the Siegfried Line. The Sergeant and his unit remained in their exposed position for eight hours, despite heavy artillery, mortar fire, and hand grenades thrown by enemy infantry at close range. At the end of eight hours, Sgt. Gerstung was still at his gun, but every other member of his squad was either wounded or killed. When he ran out of ammunition, he dashed across the ground under fire to a disabled US tank to get more .50-cal. ammunition. He continued to fight on alone until the water jacket on his machine gun barrel was pierced and the gun jammed.

Undaunted, Sgt. Gerstung crawled 50yds to another of his company's machine guns. The crew had been killed, but the Sergeant faced the enemy and continued covering the infantry assault. Soon after, an enemy tank approached his position and fired an armor-piercing round. Incredibly, the shell ripped off Sgt. Gerstung's glove but did no further damage.

Finally, when the attacking infantry was ordered to fall back, Sgt. Gerstung remained with his machine gun, giving the only covering fire for the withdrawing infantry. When all the infantry had withdrawn, the Sergeant stood, picked up his heavy machine gun, cradled it in his arms, and calmly looped an ammunition belt over his shoulder. He then slowly walked to the rear, firing short bursts at the enemy as he went.

Technical Sergeant Robert E. Gerstung is shown after receiving the Medal of Honor from President Truman in September 1945. The combination of full-size medal at the throat and a ribbon bar on the chest would only have been worn at the Medal of Honor presentation. At other times, the light blue ribbon alone would be added to the ribbon array. (NARA)

This photograph shows typical American infantrymen engaged on the Siegfried Line in the winter of 1944–45. These men wear the inadequate Parsons jacket with significant layering of other clothing underneath. M1944 "shoe paces", however, have been issued to replace the more common uninsulated leather combat boots. (NARA)

Just as Sgt. Gerstung approached friendly lines, he was struck in the leg by a mortar fragment. Unwilling to abandon his machine gun despite his injuries, he dragged himself and his machine gun the last hundred yards to the 79th Division's lines. His injuries prevented him from participating with his regiment, the 313th Infantry, in the desperate defense of the lines against the attempted German breakout several weeks later, where Sgt. Bertoldo (see page 30) of the 42nd Division would distinguish himself.

Sgt. Gerstung recovered from his wounds and survived the war. On September 5, 1945, he received the Medal of Honor. He died at the age of 63 on June 17, 1979, and is buried at Arlington National Cemetery.

Sergeant Francis Currey

Back on September 10, 1944, the US 30th Infantry Division had reached the Meuse River, which they crossed and quickly found themselves facing the vaunted Siegfried Line. After hard fighting in the Aachen Gap, the division moved southward as the Germans began their Ardennes offensive, soon to be called the Battle of the Bulge.

In December, the Allies were poised to invade the German heartland. Despite the cold and snow, the American armies looked forward to Christmas and a quick end to the war.

Hitler, however, had other plans: one last massive offensive, to push through the Ardennes region and to catch Montgomery's 21st Army unawares. In complete secrecy, 25 divisions had been scraped together to launch a surprise attack on the Allied armies advancing toward Germany. Pivotal to the plan was the capture of the bridges over the Meuse River to give passage to the Panzers. This job was assigned to the elite 1st and 12th SS Panzer Divisions, and the 12th Volksgrenadier Division. One of Hitler's favorites, Lieutenant-Colonel Otto Skorzeny, was given a brigade to spearhead the assault using American vehicles, or, since American vehicles were in short supply, German vehicles painted green with white stars. A special commando unit of English-speaking Germans, dressed in American uniforms, was readied to engage in sabotage and spread general confusion in the Malmedy area.

Because massive traffic jams behind the lines caused severe delays in reaching their initial

Sergeant Francis Currey displays the weapons he used in almost single-handedly stopping a German advance during the Battle of the Bulge. Sgt. Currey holds a Browning Automatic Rifle (BAR). In the foreground, left to right, are a .30-cal. machine gun, .50-cal. heavy machine gun, M1 Garand rifle, and bazooka. (NARA)

A very young-looking Sgt. Currey is supported by two beefy comrades in this light-hearted picture. Sgt. Currey's achievement added greatly to the luster of his regiment, the 120th Infantry, a unit descended from the 1st North Carolina Infantry, which had participated in the famous Pickett's charge at Gettysburg over 80 years before. (NARA)

objectives, 1st SS Panzer arrived at the bridges a crucial two days behind schedule. Taking Malmedy proved more difficult than the Germans expected. The Germans believed Malmedy to be lightly defended, when in actuality it was held by most of a division, the US 30th. The weather, however, favored the German assault; Allied aircraft were grounded by storms and overcast skies, nullifying their overwhelming air superiority.

By December 19, the 30th held 17 miles along the American line, including Malmedy. This area was not heavily defended because American military planners had judged the terrain unsuitable for armored vehicles. On December 21, 1944, the 1st SS Panzer Division had managed to break through a gap in the US lines and had captured a large petrol dump. That day, Skorzeny's Brigade approached Malmedy, and several of his tanks reached US positions in the town. The situation was crucial; the German advance could not be allowed to reach the bridges over the Meuse. At this juncture, a young sergeant who had seen his first combat only three months earlier would show extraordinary courage and resourcefulness.

Sgt. Francis Currey was serving as an automatic rifleman with Company K, 120th Infantry, 30th Division. On December 21, he was guarding a strong point near Malmedy. Despite a heavy US artillery bombardment and outlying tank destroyers and antitank guns, several German tanks of Col. Skorzeny's Panzer Brigade 150 broke through and forced the defenders of Sgt. Currey's strong point to retreat to a factory building nearby. Sgt. Currey found an abandoned bazooka on the factory floor but could not find ammunition anywhere. Running across the street under heavy fire, he was able to secure bazooka rounds and set himself up with a comrade in an improvised position. An enemy tank and supporting infantry were sheltering in and around a house a short distance away. Sgt. Currey risked a bazooka shot at the tank, despite the heavy fire coming from all directions. Partially exposing himself, he fired a rocket at one of the tanks and scored a direct hit. Working his way around to a new position, he took his automatic rifle and shot three Germans standing in the doorway of another house. Observing that the house, which lay on the flank of his battalion's position, was full of Germans, Sgt. Currey and his companion decided to attempt to destroy the house with bazooka fire. After arranging for covering fire, they inched up to within 50yds of the house. As soon as the covering fire began, Sgt. Currey stood up and fired, knocking down half of one wall of the house.

From his advanced position, he could see a group of five GIs who had been pinned down for several hours by three enemy tanks and the German infantry in the house. Looking around, Sgt. Currey saw a vehicle across the road which contained anti-tank rockets which he would need if the attack on the three tanks were to be successful. Under a hail of fire from both the house and the tanks, he ran across the street to the vehicle and returned unharmed with an armful of rockets. He used these with such skill that he soon forced the Panzer crews from their vehicles and into the house.

Sgt. Currey then ran to a half-track abandoned in full view of the house, and clambering onto the top, turned the heavy machine gun to fire on the house. This position proved to be too exposed, however, and he made his way to a silent American machine gun position. The crew was dead, but Sgt. Currey managed to get the gun working and continued his one-man attack on the house. So intense was his fire that the five trapped US soldiers were able to withdraw safely and soon the Germans were forced from their position, leaving their tanks behind. The Battalion's flank had been saved and five soldiers rescued by Sgt. Currey's daring and extraordinary skill with a variety of infantry weapons.

For his bravery of that day, Sgt. Currey was awarded the Medal of Honor, which he received on August 17, 1945. His other awards included the Silver Star, the Bronze Star, and three Purple Hearts. He survived the war and is one of a dwindling handful of living WWII Medal of Honor recipients.

Master Sergeant Vito R. Bertoldo

When the 42nd "Rainbow Division" arrived at the front in December 1944 the 7th Army was spread very thinly over its line, their numbers severely depleted from sending reinforcements to the fighting in the Ardennes sector to the north. The 42nd were split up and spread over the countryside in a piecemeal fashion, divided into small elements and doled out as replacements over a 90-mile front north of Strasbourg. Along this line the 1st Battalion of the 242nd Infantry had been detailed to a quiet sector around the town of Hatten.

On January 9 at 0500 hrs, the 1st Battalion's idyllic existence abruptly came to an end. Hatten and the nearby village of Rittershoffen became the focus of the massive German New Year's offensive, Operation NORDWIND. The Germans, advancing under cover of snow, suddenly released a massive artillery barrage, and then sent in the Panzers. The Germans were soon in the town and a savage house-to-house fight began. The defenders had to fight without tank or artillery support for 12 long hours. An Allied company commander arrived with orders to hold at all costs. As soon as the order was given, the officer was wounded by an artillery shell, and was taken prisoner along with a number of men of the 1st Battalion. After the war, the Captain was surprised to see a familiar face in the newspaper, that of his only disciplinary problem – Vito Bertoldo, a cook who could not get along with the mess sergeant. He had sent the cook to guard the Battalion Command Post to be rid of him, and not only had that cook escaped capture, but he had been awarded the Medal of Honor.

On the morning of January 9, Sergeant Vito Bertoldo had other things than medals to think about, primarily his own survival. His battalion's lines had been breached by the Germans and as they approached his command post, Sgt. Bertoldo left the shelter of the building and set up a machine gun in the road to prevent German infantrymen from removing mines from the roadbed. In the event, he remained in this exposed position for 12 hours, despite 88mm, machine gun, and small arms fire. Finally he was forced back inside the building, where he strapped his machine gun to a table and began to fire out the window. He engaged an enemy tank at a range of 75yds and was thrown across the room by the impact of an incoming 88mm tank round. Although dazed, Sgt. Bertoldo managed to shoot the tank commander when he popped up to survey the damage his shell had done.

When two enemy armored personnel carriers supported by a tank approached Sgt. Bertoldo's position, the Sergeant waited coolly until the Germans got out of the troop carrier before leaning out the window and mowing down over 20 Germans despite putting himself in direct fire at close range from the tank.

Sgt. Bertoldo stayed in the building to cover the retreat of the command post personnel when they evacuated to another building. He remained there alone all night. The next morning, the Sergeant took his machine gun and relocated to an adjacent command post and defended it for the entire day. He broke up the attack of an 88mm self-propelled gun supported by a tank and 15 infantrymen. Later another tank came up to the building sheltering Sgt. Bertoldo, its muzzle inches from the window, and fired point-blank. He was knocked down by a concussion, while several others in the room were severely wounded. He bounded back to his machine gun in time to spray the retreating Germans after an American bazooka had set the self-propelled gun afire.

As this command post was being prepared for evacuation, a ferocious onslaught of tanks and heavy guns intervened. Despite the barrage, Sgt. Bertoldo held off the advancing Germans by throwing white phosphorus grenades until the Germans broke off the attack. Another round, fired by

Master Sergeant Vito Bertoldo is shown in this heavily retouched official wartime photo. This photo was most likely taken in early 1945, soon after his action at Hatten, France, but well before the award of the Medal of Honor, which took place in January 1946. (NARA)

In World War I, the 42nd "Rainbow Division" was a highly decorated unit led by a young Gen. MacArthur. One of the last three American divisions activated for World War II, men of the 42nd were rushed into battle in September 1944, untried men hastily pushed into the line as replacements. (NARA)

a tank just 50yds away, threw him across the room, destroying his machine gun. Undeterred, he grabbed a rifle and remained long enough to cover the retreat of his comrades. Then he, too, made his escape.

In all, Sgt. Bertoldo had been in constant action for 48 hours and had killed at least 40 Germans and wounded many more. His stubborn resistance to overwhelming force was mirrored all along the line, where the American divisions held regardless of the force exerted against them. Both armies fought until exhausted. The Germans pulled back across the Rhine on January 25, leaving only one stubborn center of resistance on the French side of the river, the Colmar Pocket.

The 1st Battalion, 242nd Infantry was relieved on January 11, having two-thirds of its officers and men killed, wounded, or missing. The Battalion earned a Distinguished Unit Citation for this action as well as a new respect from the Germans as a foe to be reckoned with.

Sgt. Bertoldo recovered from his wounds and was awarded the Medal of Honor exactly one year after the action at Hatten. He eventually moved to California, and he is buried in the Golden Gate Cemetery in San Bruno, California.

Second Lieutenant Audie Leon Murphy

While the German's last-ditch offensives in the Ardennes and much of Alsace wore down, the southern flank of the US Seventh Army was still heavily involved in operations in the Colmar Pocket, which remained a stubborn bulge in the Allied line near the Swiss border.

Attached to the 7th Army, the 3rd Infantry Division had fought its way from North Africa, Sicily, and Anzio and then on to Operation ANVIL, later renamed DRAGOON, the invasion of southern France. Coming ashore at St. Tropez in August 1944, it advanced through the Rhone Valley, across the Vosges Mountains, and reached the Rhine by November 1944. In late January 1945, the 3rd Division was assigned to secure the Bois de Riedwihr, a forest in the northern sector of the Colmar Pocket. These woods were the key to taking the German stronghold at Holtzwihr.

On January 23, 1945, the 30th Infantry managed to take the woods and approached the outskirts of Holtzwihr. They were stopped by savage resistance involving 10 Panzers supported by 100 infantry. Badly cut up, the 30th withdrew and turned the task over to the 15th Infantry, who were ordered to take Holtzwihr the next day. The 15th encountered heavy resistance and suffered enormous casualties. Before reaching its jumping-off point, Company B lost 102 of its 120 men and all its officers except the newly promoted Second Lieutenant Audie Leon Murphy.

To say that Murphy grew up poor is a gross understatement. The seventh of twelve children, Murphy was ten years old when his father abandoned his family during the cruel Depression years. Murphy quit grade school to care for his sickly mother, Josie, and siblings. A crack shot with a rifle, the family survived on the wild game Murphy bagged. His mother died when he was 16 years old and he was determined to support his five younger siblings. When the US entered the war, Murphy saw military pay as a resource to feed his family.

Rejected by the Marine Corps and the Navy due to his age, the Army took the baby-faced, 5'7", half-starved Texan and tried to make him a cook. However, his sharp-shooting skills paid off and he headed into the infantry. "Little Texas", as his comrades called

(continued on page 41)

The US Army Medal of Honor

This Plate shows the first Medal of Honor awarded in World War II, which went to Second Lieutenant Alexander R. Nininger, Jr. The Medal is of the earlier style associated with World War I in its ribbon suspension arrangement. In World War I, the Medal was usually worn above the left breast pocket suspended from a 2½ to 3in. blue ribbon with 13 woven white stars. In World War II the predominant method of wear for the Medal of Honor became the neck ribbon.

Private Nicholas Minue; Tunisia, April 28, 1943

Colonel Leon Johnson; Benghazi, Libya, August 1943

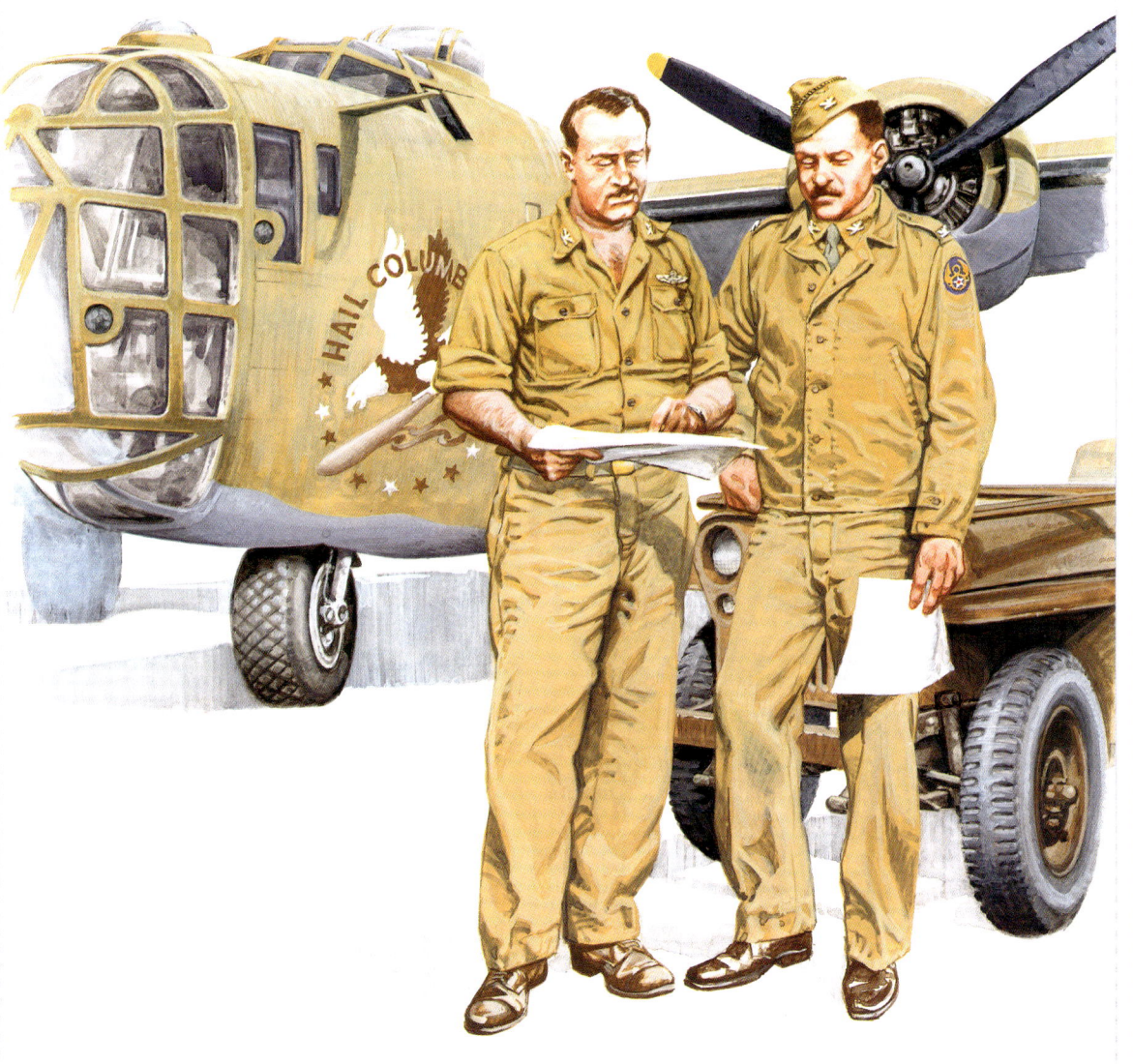

Corporal Charles Kelly; Altavilla, Italy, September 1943

D

Sergeant Thomas Baker; Saipan, June 19, 1944

E

Sergeant Maynard Smith; over the English Channel, May 1, 1943

F

Sergeant Francis Currey;
Malmedy, Belgium, December 21, 1944

G

Private Carlton W. Barrett; Normandy, June 6, 1944

him, fought on battlefields and was wounded three times, one bullet shattering his right hip. After a bout with gangrene, he returned to his company limping but determined to fight.

The remnants of Company B with "Little Texas" were in position 600yds into the woods north of the village of Holtzwihr, France. Before dawn, they moved to a position facing the village with orders to hold until relieved.

At dawn, reinforcements showed up in the form of two M10 tank destroyers of the 601st Tank Destroyer Battalion. One tank destroyer was deployed to protect the company's right flank, while the other was deployed 40yds to the company's front. Lt. Murphy knew that he had to hold his position at all costs, since a successful German advance would threaten the entire 3rd Division position.

At 1400 hrs, six German Panzers accompanied by 250 elite Mountain troops came out of Holtzwihr under cover of a fierce artillery barrage. Shells fired by the two American tank destroyers merely bounced off the heavy armor of the advancing Panzers. 88mm shells from one of the Panzers quickly incapacitated one tank destroyer and one of Company B's machine guns. Undeterred, the remaining tank destroyer moved in to the attack, firing its .30- and .50-cal. machine guns at the advancing infantry, but while rapidly maneuvering, the tank destroyer went out of control and pitched into a ditch. Lying at an acute angle, its guns unable to fire, the tank destroyer became an easy target for the artillery and advancing enemy tanks; its crew made a hasty retreat to the forest.

Having lost both tank destroyers, Lt. Murphy realized that his men could no longer hold the position. He ordered them to take cover in the trees, while he stayed to direct artillery fire on the advancing Germans. Standing under a tree in full view of the enemy, Lt. Murphy called down accurate artillery fire inflicting severe casualties, but still the advance continued. When he ran out of carbine ammunition, the Germans were a mere 50yds away.

Discarding his empty carbine but holding on to his field telephone, Lt. Murphy vaulted onto one of the disabled tank destroyers, which was burning fiercely. He brought the tank destroyer's .50-cal. machine gun to bear on the advancing Germans, who were now only 10yds away. Lt. Murphy kept up such hot fire that the Panzers, deprived of infantry support, withdrew to the tree line. Two 88mm Panzer rounds struck Lt. Murphy's tank destroyer, shaking him up but failing to stop the punishing fire he continued to pour down on the enemy.

When AAF fighter bombers appeared unexpectedly, Lt. Murphy phoned the artillery to mark the German positions with smoke. Thus aided, the aircraft executed determined strafing runs, but could not stop the German advance. In desperation, he called down artillery fire on top of his own one-man strong point. Finally, the Germans began to fall back.

In this 1945 official Army photograph, Second Lieutenant Audie Murphy looks very much the movie star he was soon to become. On his summer service dress uniform, he wears only some of the ribbons to which he was entitled. In all, he was awarded 33 decorations, including every US Army award for bravery. (NARA)

Totally exposed to German fire, Lt. Murphy had to swing the .50-cal. machine gun around 180 degrees to keep firing at the enemy who practically surrounded him. An eyewitness said, "I could see their (German) white machine gun tracers smash against the hull and turret and then glance off… I don't understand yet how he came through it alive… Flames burst from the hatches and the whole tank destroyer was sometimes wrapped in billows of smoke."

Bloody and blackened from smoke, Lt. Murphy held off the enemy for an hour until his ammunition was spent. In his autobiography, written as if the events were happening currently, he described what happened next: "As if under the influence of some drug, I slide off the tank destroyer and, without once looking back, walk down the road through the forest. If the Germans want to shoot me, let them. I am too weak from fear and exhaustion to care."

As Lt. Murphy entered the tree line, the woods shook when the tank destroyer he had just left exploded. The fire had reached the ammunition and fuel aboard.

Refusing medical treatment, Lt. Murphy immediately organized a counterattack. He and his 18 men charged with renewed vigor and retook their old position before halting to re-group. They held their position, frozen and exhausted, through the snowy January night. The next day reinforcements arrived and Holtzwihr fell.

Less than four months later, the war in Europe was over and now First Lieutenant Audie Murphy, the humble man who said the true heroes were the soldiers who had not come home, found himself the most decorated American soldier of WWII. His awards included the Medal of Honor, Distinguished Service Cross, Silver Star with oak leaf cluster (second award), Legion of Merit, Bronze Star with "V" and oak leaf cluster, Purple Heart with second oak leaf cluster (third award), Combat Infantry Badge, and four French and one Belgian award.

Arriving home, Lt. Murphy found his face on the cover of *Life* magazine and millions of people clamoring to get a glimpse of the hero. Actor James Cagney invited the civilian Murphy to Hollywood where he eventually made 44 films, mostly Westerns. His autobiography, *To Hell and Back*, released in 1949, rose to the bestseller lists and is a moving account of the life and thoughts of a front-line soldier. In 1955, the film adaptation was released with baby-faced Murphy portraying himself a decade younger.

Murphy also wrote poetry and songs recorded by top performers. He was inducted into the Country Music and Cowboy Halls of Fame. The state of Texas celebrates his birthday, June 20, as Audie Murphy Day. Hospitals, libraries, and schools bear his name and even a rose was dedicated to him. His family maintains the non-profit Audie Murphy Research Foundation.

On a foggy Memorial Day weekend in 1971, Murphy boarded a private plane to take him and five others, including the pilot, to a business meeting. The plane crashed into a Virginia mountainside, killing all on impact.

Buried at Arlington National Cemetery, Murphy's grave is the second-most visited after that of President John F. Kennedy. The cemetery had to build a flagstone walkway to his grave-site to accommodate the number of visitors paying their respects to this US hero.

First Sergeant Leonard A. Funk, Jr.

By December 1944, the Allies looked confidently to the imminent collapse of the Third Reich. The Germans, however, had other plans. When the Germans broke through the thin US lines in the Ardennes on December 16, 1944, the 82nd Airborne Division was in reserve after having taken part in two major actions, D-Day and MARKET-GARDEN, in the previous six months.

Two airborne divisions, the 82nd and 101st, were immediately sent in from reserve, the 101st to Bastogne and the 82nd to Werbomont to contain the northern shoulder of the Bulge. The 508th Parachute Infantry Regiment, one of three such regiments in the 82nd Airborne Division, moved in on December 18 and was at Chevron by the 19th. They held the line until December 24, when they were ordered to fall back to establish new lines. Although the order to "tidy up" the lines had come from Montgomery's headquarters, the paratroopers resented having to fall back; it would, in fact, be several weeks before they would be able to regain the ground they were giving up.

On January 7, the 508th undertook a large assault through knee-deep snow to attack Their-du-Mont, taking heavy casualties which resulted in them being placed in reserve for two weeks. Back in the line on January 21, 1945, the regiment remained in continuous action until February 22. During this period of intense action, First Sergeant Leonard A. Funk, Jr., of the Regiment's Company C, distinguished himself as a soldier with a quick brain and an even quicker trigger finger.

On January 29, the 508th was completing a 15-mile advance with an attack on Holzheim, Belgium. Sgt. Funk had been detailed to replace the wounded company executive officer in addition to his first sergeant's duties. The fighting was so heavy that he found himself organizing a group of headquarters clerks into a hastily improvised combat unit and then leading them, along with another platoon, in a frontal assault on 15 houses, against direct artillery fire and heavy small arms fire. Despite a driving snowstorm with waist-deep snowdrifts, the attack was a success and Sgt. Funk found himself with 30 German prisoners at no losses to his unit. Fifty more prisoners were soon added to the group left with Sgt. Funk as the battle rolled past. With no men to spare, Sgt. Funk ordered four of his clerks to remain behind and guard the prisoners in the back garden of one of the houses they had just taken.

Sgt. Funk led the rest of his men in mopping up pockets of resistance, but upon encountering a fierce and determined resistance, he withdrew to warn the men he had left behind. Before he could return, however, a strong enemy patrol had come upon Sgt. Funk's four clerks, who thought they were the expected relief from B Company. The Germans had, in fact, already captured the men from B Company, and soon captor and prisoner

First Sergeant Leonard Funk receives the Medal of Honor from President Harry Truman on a hot September day in 1945 in Washington, D.C. Sgt. Funk wears the Combat Infantryman's Badge below his ribbon bar and Paratrooper's Qualification, "Jump" Wings, above the ribbons. His shoulder patch is that of the 82nd, "All American", Airborne Division. (NARA)

had reversed roles. The recently freed Germans re-armed and prepared to attack Company C in the rear.

When Sgt. Funk walked into the yard, he did not realize the situation, since the men he saw, both prisoners and guards, were all dressed in white snow smocks. A German officer quickly strode up to him and pressed a pistol into his midsection, ordering him to surrender. Sgt. Funk pretended to comply, slowly easing his Thompson submachine gun from his shoulder. Suddenly Sgt. Funk leveled his weapon and fired at the officer at point-blank range. At the same time, he called to the captured GIs to retrieve their weapons and join in the fight. The remaining Germans returned fire, killing the man standing next to Sgt. Funk. In less than a minute the action was over; the US paratroopers were free and 21 Germans lay dead, with another 24 wounded.

In late February 1945, the 508th was taken out of the line, and by April they were sent, first to Chartres, France, ready to rescue Allied prisoners-of-war if the opportunity arose, and then on to Frankfurt-am-Main, where they remained until the war ended.

Sgt. Funk, who had been decorated for action in Normandy and in Holland during Operation MARKET-GARDEN, received the Medal of Honor for his action in Belgium on August 23, 1945.

Returning home, Leonard Funk went back to his prewar clerical job. In 1947, he joined the Veterans' Administration, eventually retiring as Division Chief of the Pittsburgh Regional Office in 1972. He died of cancer in 1992, and is buried in Arlington National Cemetery.

Technical Sergeant Beaufort T. Anderson

As early as the end of 1943, the Ryukyu Islands were identified as a possible invasion site on the road to the Japanese Home Islands. In October 1944, the Joint Chiefs of Staff decided to invade Okinawa in the Ryukyu chain. Operation ICEBERG, as the invasion was code-named, would be the first invasion of Japanese territory proper, since Okinawa was a prefecture, albeit a distant one, of the Home Islands. This first invasion of Japanese home territory goes far to explain the ferocious resistance encountered; only 7,500 of an estimated 115,000 defenders were taken alive. Henceforth, Allied planners were forced to reassess the cost likely to be incurred in the invasion of Japan itself, scheduled for November 1945.

The 96th Infantry Division was one of four Army divisions chosen for ICEBERG, in which they were to be assisted by the III Marine Amphibious

The winter of 1944–45 was extremely cold and snowy in the Ardennes. The GIs kept warm with whatever clothing they could obtain. Two of the central figures in this photo wear the M1944 field jacket, while most of the others wear the woolen overcoat. All have been lucky enough to procure the cold weather "shoe pacs". (NARA)

Corps, consisting of three Marine divisions. The 96th was a division of the Organized Reserve, one of the "draftee divisions", composed primarily of men drafted after Pearl Harbor. The division was organized in 1943, spent two years in training, and arrived in mid-1944 to join General MacArthur's XXIV Corps in Australia. In October of that year, the men of the 96th took an active part in the invasion of Leyte in the Philippines.

In the action to come, the bloodiest in the Pacific war, the Army and Marine Corps would lose almost 14,000 men. The 96th, which suffered more casualties than any of the other three Army divisions, was given some of the most difficult assignments and they handled them with "violence, resolution, and skill". By this time, action in the Pacific could become violent and very personal as the Americans employed tank-infantry-demolition teams to root out tenacious, well-dug-in Japanese whose only ambition was to kill as many Americans as possible before they themselves died. "Corkscrew and blow torch fighting" the commanding general called it.

The invasion began on schedule, on Sunday, April 1, 1945. The northern half of the island fell quickly, and all went well until the Army hit a series of concentric defensive belts protecting Shuri, Okinawa's second largest urban area. Kakazu Ridge formed part of one of the outer defenses. Here, on April 10, the advance bogged down. For the next three days, the Japanese staged a savage series of counterattacks, preceded by an extremely heavy 5-hour mortar barrage, but after much hard fighting the counterattacks were beaten off and the American advance continued.

On the third day of these brutal Japanese counterattacks on Kakazu Ridge, Staff Sergeant Beauford T. Anderson of the 381st Infantry Regiment, 96th Division, won one of five Medals of Honor awarded to men of the 96th for service on Okinawa. Sgt. Anderson, a veteran of the Leyte invasion, had already been awarded the Bronze Star for running 50yds under fire to rescue two wounded men.

After withstanding two nights of terror and death, Sgt. Anderson ordered his exhausted men into shelter in cave-like tombs carved into the rock of the ridge on the third night of the Kakazu Ridge attacks. Having done so, he was faced with a sudden rush of Japanese into his position. He emptied his magazine into the advancing enemy and in the resulting confusion seized an unexploded Japanese mortar round and threw it into the enemy's midst to gain time to reload. When the shell exploded, killing several of the attackers, Sgt. Anderson spied a box of mortar shells and, ripping off the top, took one out, removed the safety pin, and struck it against a rock to arm it. He threw it and once again killed several Japanese. Seeing this as his only chance, Sgt. Anderson alternated between carbine fire and mortar bombs until the enemy withdrew. In all, the sergeant killed 25 Japanese and destroyed several machine guns and knee mortars. Although seriously wounded, Sgt. Anderson then reported the action to his company

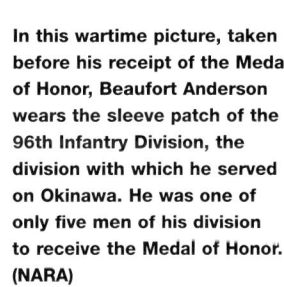

In this wartime picture, taken before his receipt of the Medal of Honor, Beaufort Anderson wears the sleeve patch of the 96th Infantry Division, the division with which he served on Okinawa. He was one of only five men of his division to receive the Medal of Honor. (NARA)

The rough, hilly terrain on Okinawa provided the Japanese defenders with many opportunities for concealment. Here, a US tank equipped with a flame-throwing device neutralizes a Japanese strongpoint in one of the island's many caves. Flame-throwers and explosives had to be employed extensively in this rugged terrain. (NARA)

commander, over the strenuous objections of his men who thought that he had already done enough.

The battle for Shuri continued until the end of May, when after extraordinarily bloody fighting, the Japanese evacuated the area. The southern part of the island was not fully pacified, however, until the end of June 1945.

Sgt. Anderson's wounds kept him out of action for the rest of the war, but on Memorial Day 1946, Sgt. Anderson, now a technical sergeant, was presented with the Medal of Honor at a ceremony on the White House lawn.

After the war, "Andy" Anderson moved from his native Wisconsin to California, where he remained active in the Army Reserve, rising to the rank of second lieutenant before his wartime wounds forced his retirement. He spent his retirement running a cattle ranch and engaging in local politics. He was elected Mayor, and twice a City Councilman, of Seaside, California, as well as three times Monterey County Supervisor, with one term as Chairman.

He died at the age of 74 in November 1996, with few in California aware that he was a Medal of Honor recipient. However, when the Army was notified of his death in late 2000, arrangements were made to re-inter Lt. Anderson and his wife with full honors at Arlington National Cemetery.

ARMY AIR FORCE
Sergeant Maynard H. Smith

In January 1943 at the Casablanca Conference, Churchill and Roosevelt agreed that Combined Bomber Operations would carry the air war to the German industrial heartland. Effective bomber operations against Germany's production capabilities were seen as an indispensable precursor to a successful land invasion of Europe. The US Army Air Forces (AAF) would conduct precision daylight operations while RAF Bomber Command would concentrate on night-time area bombing.

The planners of Combined Bomber Operations could not have foreseen the cost in men and machines. The air campaign over Europe cost proportionally more casualties than any other. In the year of its inception, AAF casualties were running at 30 percent a month, making successful completion of 25 missions, the requisite number for rotation out of combat, a long-shot indeed. Morale was at a low point and a hero was needed. Fate supplied one in May 1943.

Maynard H. Smith was the first enlisted man in the US 8th Air Force to be awarded the Medal of Honor. So short and slight that he acquired the nickname "Snuffy" after a popular comic strip character, Sgt. Smith as a 32-year-old air gunner on his first mission seemed an unlikely hero. Having joined the Army as the result of a choice between a jail term for nonpayment of child support and the Army, Sgt. Smith felt little enthusiasm for military life. By volunteering for air gunner training, he obtained the automatic rank of sergeant and went off to Texas for training. In early 1943, he arrived in England and was assigned to the 423rd Bombardment Squadron, 306th Bomb Group of the 8th Air Force as a B-17 air gunner.

On May 1, 1943, Sgt. Smith boarded B-17 649 for his first mission, a raid on the U-boat base at St. Nazaire, and found himself in the ball turret as England slowly slipped away beneath him. The ball turret was a Plexiglas half-sphere sticking out into the open sky under the belly of the B-17, the most exposed position in the aircraft – the so-called "suicide seat". Sgt. Smith, locked into his bubble with two .50-cal. machine guns, defended the underside of his aircraft as it began to fly through flak on the way to its target.

The ever-cocky 5'3" B-17 gunner, Sergeant Maynard "Snuffy" Smith was the first enlisted man in the Eighth Air Force to receive the Medal of Honor. Sgt. Smith is dressed in the fleece-lined leather flying suit made necessary by the unheated bombers which flew at altitudes where the air temperature was often –60 degrees Fahrenheit. (NARA)

Over the target, severe flak and fighters brought down a large proportion of the attacking bombers, and a navigation error on the return trip brought the battered formation over the heavily defended French port city of Brest. Two more "Flying Fortresses" in the formation were brought down by flak, and German fighters pursued Sgt. Smith's aircraft out over the English Channel. There was an explosion, caused by the rupture of gasoline tanks. The ensuing fire raged uncontrollably in the radio compartment and the waist. The radio operator and both waist gunners bailed out immediately, leaving Sgt. Smith with the severely wounded tail gunner, who had dragged himself into the waist of the B-17. The aircraft's intercom was knocked out and the radio compartment fire prevented communication with the pilot, co-pilot, engineer, and navigator in the forepart of the plane. Unable to discover the situation of the remainder of the crew, the pilot continued the flight back to England despite the raging inferno behind him.

Meanwhile, Sgt. Smith was left alone, flames all around, with a raging fire, a wounded comrade and attacking German fighters all calling for his immediate attention. With all these urgent concerns, he did what had to be done by attending alternately to each of these compelling demands. First he treated the tail gunner, and then drove off an attacking German aircraft, and only then could he turn his

In this undoubtedly staged photograph, Sgt. Smith is shown peeling potatoes as punishment for missing a mission briefing. This is how Sgt. Smith was found on the day he was to receive the Medal of Honor from the Secretary of War, who had flown in from the States for the presentation. (NARA)

attention to the fires consuming his aircraft. The radio compartment fire, fueled to incredible heat by the leaking oxygen released by the ruptured oxygen system, was so intense that it melted the radio, camera, and even a gun mount. Exploding ammunition also had to be jettisoned; Smith had a choice of several large holes burned into the skin of the aircraft out of which to throw the endangered ammunition. Once again a renewed fighter attack called Sgt. Smith back to his guns and then immediately back to the fire. Soon the aircraft's firefighting equipment was expended and Sgt. Smith, wrapping himself in some clothing, finally extinguished the fires by literally stamping them out with his body. Somehow, the aircraft stayed together long enough to land in England.

An elaborate ceremony was planned, with Secretary of War Henry Stimson making the award of the Medal of Honor to "Snuffy" Smith. Shortly before the ceremony, however, Sgt. Smith was found performing KP as punishment for missing a mission briefing, a situation the journalists covering the ceremony found irresistible. The *New York Times* dubbed him the "[Potato] Peeler Bomber".

After receiving the Medal of Honor, Sgt. Smith flew five more missions, and then took a desk job in England. He was discharged in 1945, and returned to a job with the Internal Revenue Service in D.C. There he ran afoul of the Food and Drug Administration for selling a "misbranded" medication, a forerunner of Viagra, which he called "Firmo". A series of unsuccessful business ventures followed until Snuffy Smith finally bought and operated *The Police Officers Journal*, a successful daily newspaper in New York City. He retired to Florida in 1976 and died in 1984 at the age of 72.

Colonel Leon W. Johnson

In early 1943, Army Air Force strategic planners projected that the German Luftwaffe posed a grave threat to their two most important strategic objectives: the bombing of German industry and the much-discussed land invasion of Europe. Destruction of the oilfields and refinery facilities at Ploesti in Romania (the source of over 30 percent of German fuel requirements) was chosen as the most feasible method of reducing the combat effectiveness of the Luftwaffe. Studies indicated, however, that traditional high-altitude bombardment would require over 1,000 heavy bombers in nine missions of 120 planes each, far more aircraft than could be supplied at that time. With the knowledge that in June 1942, 13 B-24s had successfully attacked Ploesti and encountered only relatively weak defenses, Roosevelt approved a massive attack on Ploesti at the Casablanca Conference of January 1943, assigning planning to General Henry "Hap" Arnold in March of that year.

There were significant difficulties but little time standing between the planners and successful execution of their ambitious plan. Chief among these, but not fully appreciated at the time, were the heavy German defenses around Ploesti: massive flak towers, over 200 heavy anti-aircraft guns, two Luftwaffe fighter bases nearby, barrage balloons, and an effective radar detection net. The planners decided upon a single, treetop-level assault to be conducted by B-24 bombers of the 9th Air Force flying from Benghazi, Libya; it was hoped that a low-altitude attack would take the Germans by surprise and evade radar surveillance. What the planners did not know was that the Germans had broken the 9th Air Force communication code and the bombers would be expected.

Five bombardment groups of 30–36 aircraft each were assigned to the mission: the 376th led by Col. Keith Compton, the 93rd with Lt Col. Addison Baker, the 98th with Col. John Kane, the 44th with Col. Leon Johnson, and the 389th with Col. John Wood, under the overall command of Brig. Gen. Uzal Ent. They had just over two weeks to practice bombing a target painted on the ground, and were ready to set off on the 2,700-mile round trip to Ploesti by the end of July.

On Sunday, August 1, 1943, 178 B-24s took off from Benghazi. At first, luck was with them. While each aircraft exceeded its maximum load capacity, given the weight of 3,000 gallons of fuel, 4,000lbs of bombs, and extra armor, all but one made successful takeoffs. As they approached Greece, however, their luck changed. The aircraft carrying the lead navigator inexplicably crashed into the sea, and the aircraft carrying the alternate navigator violated procedures and went down to investigate. When the second aircraft could not regain altitude and had to turn back, the formation ploughed on without either of the only two navigators who had received special instructions for the mission.

Crossing over into Albania, the formation was stretching ever further apart, and when it reached the Pindus Mountains, it found towering cloud formations blocking the way. Group commanders chose different routes to deal with the clouds: some flew over, some through, and others under the clouds. When they came out on the other side, the formation, and the attack sequence, was badly scattered. In particular, Col. Kane and a portion of Col. Johnson's group, who had gone under the clouds, found themselves far behind.

Next, the lead group made a wrong turn at the initial point and headed for Bucharest instead of Ploesti. Once over Bucharest, the group had to recalculate their approach, forcing them to attack from the south rather than the west as planned. When they reached the target, they would be attacking at treetop level from a different direction than the other attacking aircraft, which had detected and corrected for the navigational error. To add to the confusion, upon arriving at Ploesti, Gen. Ent changed the precise attack orders to "targets of opportunity", even ordering one attack from the north. Chaos was now assured: over 160 aircraft would be making attacks at 100 to 300ft from all directions on any targets they might chance upon.

Colonel Leon Johnson, a 1926 West Point graduate, served in the infantry for three years before deciding that "things looked more interesting from the air." He was involved with the formation of the 8th Air Force, and was one of its first four flying officers. (NARA)

Having intercepted aircraft-to-aircraft radio communications, the Germans were expecting the B-24s as they came in over the target and they opened up with concealed 88mm and 105mm anti-aircraft guns at point-blank range. Adding to the mayhem, the American delayed-action bombs began to explode on impact, creating dense smoke which obscured visibility for aircraft pilots following in to the attack. Intense flak, rolling clouds of black smoke, zero visibility, and the real possibility of collision with friendly aircraft made the raid itself a scene from hell.

As Col. Johnson and Col. Kane arrived from the south, the other groups were just finishing their attacks. They could see that the plan had gone badly wrong. The time-delayed bombs dropped by previous groups had exploded prematurely; the targets were completely obscured by billowing smoke and flame. To add to the picture, burning B-24s littered the ground, a testament to the ferocity of the German flak concentrations and fighter aircraft. Both men knew any attack would require flying blind at low level through an area menaced by high industrial chimneys and steel barrage balloon cables toward an almost invisible target, through a gauntlet of point-blank antiaircraft fire, with the ever-present danger that more time-delayed bombs would explode directly beneath them.

Both group leaders had every reason to turn back, but they both knew the importance, strategic and psychological, of the success of this raid; strategic bombing was in its infancy and the outcome of this one mission could decide its future. Both Colonels. Kane and Johnson pushed in to the attack. Col. Kane's group went in first, losing 15 of its 46 aircraft two of the aircraft being destroyed before even reaching the target.

Finally, Col. Johnson with 15 aircraft (the other 21 previously having separated to attack a target to the north) entered the smoke on the way to his assigned target, the Columbia Acquila refinery. Almost immediately, he had to take evasive action to avoid a collision with aircraft of the 376th withdrawing after their own attack. Day had turned into night, lit by the fires from the burning refineries and the flashes from the heavy AA guns firing so close below them. Chimneys and steel balloon cables pushed from their minds, Col. Johnson's fifteen crews executed the bombing run and nine came out the other side into the sunlight, leaving six of their fellows behind.

In all, the Ploesti raid cost 54 aircraft and 532 men dead, missing, or interned. In return for this loss, the Army Air Force bombers had shown themselves skilled and tenacious fighters who could achieve their objectives against overwhelming odds. In fact, this extraordinary mission produced one of the highest number of Medals of Honor for a single engagement in World War II; Col. Johnson and Col. Kane, along with three of their comrades from other groups, received their country's highest award for valor for their actions that day.

Col. Johnson survived the return trip to Benghazi, landing in his damaged aircraft 13 hours after taking off that morning. In September 1943, Col. Johnson returned to the 8th Air Force in England, where he organized and commanded the 14th Combat Wing until the end of the war. He stayed in the newly formed United States Air Force after the war, commanding the 15th Air Force in 1947. He completed several high-level headquarters assignments, and advanced to the rank of 4-star General in 1957. He retired in 1961, but continued consulting for many years. Gen. Johnson died in 1997 at the age of 93 and is buried in Arlington National Cemetery beside Lucille, his wife of 54 years.

First Lieutenant Edward S. Michael

By late 1943, losses of both aircraft and their crews were so great that the entire concept of strategic bombing was called into question. During one raid over Schweinfurt in August, 39 percent of the attacking aircraft had been lost. The effort continued, however, and slowly the balance shifted. America's industrial capability produced replacement aircraft with phenomenal efficiency, and as time went on, improved fighter aircraft allowed greater protection for the bomber formations.

The heavy bombers, primarily the B-17s of the 8th Air Force, undertook high-altitude, daytime strategic bombing missions over Germany, missions often involving more than eight hours in the air. These hours were filled with danger. First was the danger of collision as large numbers of aircraft, none of which were equipped with radar, took off with very short intervals and had to climb to a pre-arranged altitude, often through dense cloud layers, to rendezvous with the other aircraft of the formation.

The rendezvous completed, the aircraft were arranged in defensive "boxes", groups of aircraft deployed to maximize the defensive firepower of each aircraft's machine guns. One aircraft in the forward box was primarily responsible for navigation and identification of the target at the inception of the bombing run. The mission leader, in a different aircraft, made whatever tactical decisions became necessary in flight. In the event a lead plane was hit, an event by no means uncommon, another plane took over. The sequence could be repeated several times during an average mission.

Once arranged in boxes, a long period of anxious waiting, punctuated by extreme cold, followed on the way to the target. Altitudes of 30,000 feet were common, subjecting the crews to outside temperatures of minus 60 degrees Fahrenheit in unheated, unpressurized aircraft. Waist gunners stood by large, uncovered windows to man their .50-cal. machine guns. Oxygen masks and bulky clothing added to the crews' discomfort.

Crossing over into enemy-held territory brought attacks by German fighters. Tight box formations kept losses to "acceptable" levels, but stragglers in particular were quickly singled out and shot down.

Once the target was acquired and the bomb run begun, the bombers could no longer maneuver but were required to fly "straight and level" until the moment of bomb release. Most important targets were supplied with heavy anti-aircraft protection, which meant flying straight through bursts of deadly flak without any deviation from course.

After bomb release, the bombers were once again free to take evasive action to avoid the worst of the flak, but once outside the zone of flak protection, the German fighters, refueled and re-armed, renewed their attacks. The bomber formation, continually reduced by attrition, made its way back to England and safety... until the next mission.

On April 11, 1944, the 305th Bomb Group left their base at Chelveston, England, to attack a ball-bearing plant at Stettin, 75 miles beyond Berlin. First Lieutenant Edward S. Michael piloted the B-17 *"Bertie Lee"* in the rearmost box of the formation. Near Berlin the *"Bertie Lee"* suffered flak damage to the left wing, but there was much worse to follow. Four hours into the flight, the formation was swarmed by over 100 German fighter aircraft. Lt. Michael's aircraft was singled out by a group of fighters and was raked along its entire length by 20mm cannon shells, taking out two engines and most of its instruments. The *"Bertie Lee"* dropped from the formation, with several German fighters in pursuit. Their intense fusillade blew out the side cockpit window, wounding the co-pilot, smearing hydraulic fluid across the windscreen, and filling the cockpit with smoke. Seriously wounded in the thigh and unable to see ahead, Lt. Michael fought to regain control of the aircraft, which fell 3,000ft before he could level it off.

The radio operator came forward and reported that the entire bomb bay was in flames. When he had attempted to drop his load of incendiary

Roosevelt presents the award document for the Medal of Honor to First Lieutenant Edward Michael in Washington, D. C. on January 15, 1945, as his family looks on. Of interest is that Lt. Michael wears not only the full-size medal around his neck but also the ribbon for the medal on his ribbon bar. (NARA)

bombs, the release lever did not function. Realizing that the fire would soon burn through the control cables or detonate the bomb load, Lt. Michael ordered the crew to bail out. The pilot and co-pilot were preparing to bail out as well when they heard a machine gun firing from the nose. The bombardier had not been aware of the fire, and when Lt. Michael ordered him to bail out, he replied that his parachute had been shredded by cannon fire. With three men and only two parachutes, Lt. Michael decided to attempt a crash landing as far into France as possible.

First, however, he had to continue violent evasive action, despite the damage to the aircraft, until he could shake off the tenacious German fighters. After 45 minutes of constant attack, Lt. Michael dived into a cloud bank and was able to evade further pursuit. By this time the bombardier had been successful in jettisoning the incendiary bombs, but was unable to close the bomb bay doors, further slowing the aircraft which was already flying on only two engines.

Coming out of the clouds, the *"Bertie Lee"* was hit by flak and forced down to treetop level, flying right into the concentrated fire of a flak tower. Lt. Michael somehow kept his aircraft in the air across France, but at some point, he lost consciousness from loss of blood.

Lt. Michael regained consciousness just as the *"Bertie Lee"* passed the English coast, and he insisted upon resuming command. The aircraft had no landing gear, airspeed indicator, or flaps; there was little visibility

At their base at Chelveston, England, the 305th Bomb Group examines the gift of a German flag given "to avenge your losses at Schweinfort [*sic*]." Schweinfurt, Bavaria, was hit by two disastrous 8th Air Force raids in 1943. Losses among the bombers were extremely heavy; the second raid was the most costly air attack of the war. (NARA)

The B-17 was the workhorse of the American Strategic Air Offensive over Germany. A prototype flew in 1935 at an impressive 252mph. As the war progressed, each later B-17 model had greater firepower and more armor than the model before. The B-17G, deployed in 1943, had a top speed of 287mph and a service ceiling of over 35,000ft. (USAF)

through the windscreen; and the rudder and elevators were damaged. In spite of all these difficulties, the wounded Lt. Michael managed a perfect belly landing, bringing the "*Bertie Lee*" in without mishap.

It was not until January 1945 that Lt. Michael, while in Washington, D.C. to receive his Medal of Honor, would learn that the last missing crew member had been located in a prisoner-of-war camp. Despite all the hardship and danger, Lt. Michael had saved his entire crew.

Second Lieutenant Robert E. Femoyer

With the exception of the Ploesti raids, the AAF had neglected German oil production targets until early 1944, when effective fighter protection began to become available. The campaign against German synthetic oil production facilities began in earnest in mid-1944, and it soon became clear that it would be a long campaign. The Germans had allocated a tremendous labor pool to getting damaged plants rapidly back into production, and there was a constant seesaw between destruction and rebuilding, making multiple return trips to the same target a necessity. Further complicating matters, most synthetic fuel plants were located deep in the Reich and heavily protected by flak installations.

On November 2, 1944, the 447th Bomber Group was assigned the target of a synthetic oil plant at Merseburg, near Leipzig, in eastern Germany, a long 500 miles from the 447th's base at Rattlesden, England. At the target briefing that morning, a young navigator assigned to the 711th Bomber Squadron took careful notes of the tortuous course to Merseburg lined by flak concentrations all along the route.

The young navigator, Second Lieutenant Robert E. Femoyer, was preparing for his seventh mission with the 711th, having celebrated his 23rd birthday two days before. He was from Huntington, West Virginia, and had joined the Enlisted Reserve Corps at Virginia Polytechnic Institute in November 1942. Called to active duty early in 1943, he washed out of pilot training in Mississippi, but successfully completed Aerial Gunnery School and then Navigation School in Louisiana. He had arrived two months earlier at Rattlesden as a second lieutenant and was assigned as navigator to the B-17 *"L-Love"*.

The mission for the *"L-Love"* was routine until the final approach to the target. Nearing Merseburg, the aircraft was hit by several direct hits of flak, forcing it to leave the formation and begin the perilous journey home alone. Lt. Femoyer, thrown from his seat, was seriously wounded in the back and side by shrapnel. Unable to regain his seat, he persuaded crew members to prop him up and give him his maps. Mindful of the dangers of the return trip, Lt. Femoyer refused pain relievers or sedatives in order to keep his mind clear. For several hours, sitting in a pool of his own blood, the navigator safely guided his aircraft through the maze of enemy flak positions along the route back to base. The *"L-Love"* sustained no further damage, and upon reaching the safety of the English Channel, Lt. Femoyer finally permitted administration of a sedative. He died of his injuries shortly after his aircraft landed safely at Rattlesden.

A 22-year-old Second Lieutenant Robert Femoyer is shown in an unusual combination of uniform: a tan tropical tunic with an olive-drab service cap. While the tropical uniform was not common in the UK-based 8th Air Force, Lt. Femoyer had trained in the American South, attending flight training in Mississippi, gunnery school in Florida, and navigation instruction in Louisiana. (NARA)

Lt. Femoyer was killed in a raid over Merseberg, near Leipzig, in November 1944. His Medal of Honor was awarded to his parents on May 9, 1945, in a small private ceremony. The presenting officer is an unidentified Army Air Forces major-general, probably from a base near Lt. Femoyer's home of Huntington, West Virginia. (NARA)

Lt. Femoyer's self-sacrifice was acknowledged by the posthumous award of the Medal of Honor in May 1945.

Major James H. Howard

While life for bomber crews during World War II never became safe or comfortable, crew longevity increased when by late 1943 the idea of effective fighter escort for the heavy bombers became a reality. Although fighter escort for an entire round-trip was not yet feasible, the introduction of fighter squadrons equipped with P-51 Mustangs spelled the end of the "go-it-alone" role of the bomber in the 8th Air Force.

One of these new escort fighter squadrons, the 356th, attached to the 354th Fighter Group of the 9th Air Force, was sent to its base in England in December 1943, under the command of Major James H. Howard. He had taken over a squadron plagued by hard luck and had brought it to top efficiency by instilling the spirit of co-operation and camaraderie which he had learned half a world away while the US was still at peace.

"Jimmy" Howard was an American born in Canton, China, where his father was a physician, the head of the Eye Department at Peking Union Medical College. In the early 1930s, the Howard family returned to the US, where Jimmy went on to study pre-med at Pomona College. Flying, however, proved more interesting than medicine and in 1937, Jimmy applied for and passed the Navy's short course in aviation at Pensacola, Florida, becoming a carrier-qualified naval aviator. By 1941, however, the hide-bound peacetime Navy couldn't compete with the opportunity to enlist in the newly forming American Volunteer Group, or AVG, which was taking military fliers into its ranks to assist China in its war with Japan.

Vice Squadron Leader Howard flew 56 combat missions with the AVG in a 30-month period, and was credited with six kills. This relatively modest score (some AVG pilots had scores of 15 to 20 Japanese kills) was not a fair representation of the energy and activity he displayed while with the AVG. He flew a wide variety of missions, including long-range reconnaissance, bomber escort, and fighter sweeps against ground and air targets, and still had time to act as aid to the commander of the Chinese Air Force, during which time he participated in the design of the Chunking airport. Upon the death of his squadron commander, "Scarsdale" Jack Newkirk, Howard took over command of the 2nd Squadron, the Panda Bears.

When the AVG disbanded, after America's entry into the war, Jim Howard decided to take a commission in the Army Air Force rather than returning to the Navy. Upon arrival in England in December 1943, Howard, now a major, threw himself into the new fight. The next month, January 1944, he was to become known as a "one-man air force" to the bomber crews of the 8th Air Force when for more than an hour he fought off over two dozen German fighters attacking the bomber formations on their return from raids

James H. Howard, shown here as a colonel, received his Medal of Honor as a major in January 1944. On his right breast pocket he wears a Flying Tigers emblem, a remembrance of his service in China with the American Volunteer Group. Featured in several wartime publications, Col. Howard's modest style always came through. "I seen my duty and done it" was how he described his Medal of Honor winning venture to a *New York Times* reporter. (NARA)

over Germany. During the combat, the bomber crews cheered the unknown pilot on, and at debriefing the crews were effusive in their praise, crediting the pilot with six kills and the prevention of severe losses among the bombers. Over a week later, the Air Force identified Maj. Howard as the lone pilot. When the bomber crewmen found out that he had overcautiously claimed only two kills, two probables, and one damaged, they began a letter-writing campaign to the Confirmation Board to raise the score to at least six.

Investigation of the episode eventually led to the award of the Medal of Honor for the no-longer anonymous pilot. On January 11, 1944, the 354th Fighter Group had been assigned to "target support" for strategic bombing raids over Oschersleben and Halberstadt. As the bombers returned from the raid, swarmed by German fighters, Maj. Howard rejoined the formation and dispatched one flight to cover the rear "boxes" and another to the forward boxes. Then Maj. Howard himself led a flight in to join the mêlée.

Breaking away from an attack, Maj. Howard brought his aircraft back up to the bomber's altitude only to find himself alone. He immediately saw a twin-engine night fighter and, as he stated to the *New York Times* in January 1944, "went down after him, gave him several 'squirts' and watched him crash." Next he spotted a Focke Wolf 190 passing below; when the German pulled up into the sun, Maj. Howard gave him a "squirt" and almost flew into his canopy as the German bailed out. Then he followed a Messerschmidt 109 in a turning fight, scored several hits, but did not see whether his target crashed.

Climbing again to the bomber's altitude, Maj. Howard took on another 109, and then two more after that. The seemingly endless merry-go-round went on and on: regain bomber altitude, engage a German fighter, and return to the bomber formations to start again. Soon, his ammunition running low, Maj. Howard would go into the attack without using his guns, his mere presence often enough to chase off the attacker.

One hour was the allotted time for the fighters to remain with the bombers, but Maj. Howard still had one gun working when his time had expired, and he decided to continue the fight. He climbed again to come alongside the B-17s, saw a 109, and engaged it in a steep diving fight. The next time up, he saw a Dornier 217 preparing to make a rocket attack. The Major dived on the Dornier, which beat a hasty retreat without any shots being fired. Finally, completely out of ammunition, he reluctantly left action to return to base. On landing, he was amused to find that he had only one bullet hole in his aircraft.

Although Maj. Howard made little of his exploit, the bomber crews would not let the matter lie; letters poured in to the Confirmation Board and to General Jimmy Doolittle. As a result of this campaign, Gen. Doolittle upgraded his recommendation for an award from a Distinguished Flying Cross to one for the Medal of Honor. In June 1944, the award of the nation's highest combat decoration was approved for the modest flyer.

Jimmy Howard ended the war as commander of an advanced fighter training base at Pinnelas Field, Florida, and rose to the rank of brigadier-general. After leaving the service, he became a successful businessman, eventually retiring to Florida. He died in March 1995, and is buried at Arlington National Cemetery, Washington, D.C.

Major James Howard receives his Medal of Honor on June 5, 1944, from Lieutenant-General Carl Spaatz, Commanding General, US Strategic Air Forces. It is interesting to note that Maj. Howard wears only three ribbons for the presentation ceremony, while he wears six ribbons, in addition to the Medal of Honor ribbon, in the previous photograph, taken shortly after award. (NARA)

BIBLIOGRAPHY

Ambrose, Stephen E., *D-Day June 6, 1944: The Climactic Battle of World War II*, Simon & Schuster (New York, 1994)

Boston Publishing Company, ed., *Above and Beyond*, Boston Publishing Co. (Boston, 1985)

D'Este, Carlo, *World War II in the Mediterranean 1942-1945*, Algonquin Books (Chapel Hill, N.C., 1990)

Devlin, Gerard M., *Paratrooper! The Saga of U.S. Army and Marine Parachute and Glider Combat Troops During World War II*, St. Martin's (New York, 1979)

Goolrich, William K., *et al*, *Battle of the Bulge*, Time-Life Books (Alexandria, Va, 1979)

Henry, Mark R., *The US Army In World War II (2) The Mediterranean*, Men-at-Arms 347, Osprey Publishing Ltd. (Oxford, 2000)

Henry, Mark R., *The US Army In World War II (3) North-West Europe*, Men-at-Arms 350, Osprey Publishing Ltd. (Oxford, 2001)

Jablonski, Edward, *Airwar*, Doubleday Publishing (Gordon City, N.Y., 1971)

Maguire, Jon A., *Art of The Flight Jacket: Classic Leather Jackets of World War II*, Schiffer Publishing Ltd. (Atglen, 1995)

Maguire, Jon A., *Gear Up! Flight Clothing & Equipment of USAAF Airmen in World War II*, Schiffer Publishing Ltd. (Atglen, 1995)

Mikaelian, Allen, *Medal of Honor*, Hyperion Books (New York, 2002)

Neillands, Robin, *The Bomber War*, Overlook Press (Woodstock, N.Y., 2001)

Rooney, Andy, *My War*, Times Books (New York, 1995)

Smurthwaite, David, *The Pacific War Atlas 1941–1945*, Facts On File, Inc. (New York, 1995)

US Department of the Army, Center of Military History, *The Supreme Command* (Washington, D.C., 1989)

US Department of the Army, History Division, *Okinawa: The Last Battle* (Washington, D.C., 1948)

Webster, Sir Charles, *The Strategic Air Offensive against Germany 1939-1945*, HMSO (London, 1961)

THE PLATES

A: Medal of Honor
Second Lieutenant Alexander R. Nininger, Jr.

Second Lieutenant Alexander R. Nininger, Jr., a 1941 graduate of the US Military Academy at West Point, New York, was assigned to the US Army's Philippine Division in 1941. Seeing Company K under heavy enemy attack, the 23-year-old Lt. Nininger left his own unit to help in the hand-to-hand fighting. He repeatedly forced his way into the middle of battles by attacking the advancing enemy with rifle fire and hand grenades.

An inspiration to the men who saw his superhuman determination to plunge through enemy lines, his comrades caught up with him deep in what had been thought to be unreachable territory. They found his lifeless body surrounded by three dead enemy soldiers, the last men he killed before dying himself on January 12, 1942. Less than a month later, he became the first man to receive the Medal of Honor during World War II.

The nation, and especially its communities, often reveres Medal of Honor recipients in various ways. In 1944, a Coastal Transport ship was named the USS *Alexander R. Nininger* and on Memorial Day, 1994, a bronze statue commemorating the life and heroic military service of Lt. Alexander "Sandy" Nininger was dedicated in Ft. Lauderdale, Florida. Ft. Lauderdale also has named a street for Lt. Nininger, and hosts an American Veterans Post and an Army Reserve Center named for him. In January 2001, the governor of Florida opened the Sandy Nininger State Veterans Nursing Home in Pembroke Pines, Florida. In addition, the US Military Academy has named its First Division Barracks in memory of its illustrious alumnus.

B: Private Nicholas Minue; Tunisia, April 28, 1943

Operation TORCH, the invasion of Northwest Africa, began on November 8, 1942. A combined British and American force landed at Casablanca, Oran, and Algiers, with the immediate objective of taking French North Africa before Axis forces could respond. Moving east into Tunisia, the British were the first to encounter the Germans on November 17, where the advance stalled. Gen. Eisenhower committed American units to reinforce the British, but it was not enough to dislodge the Germans before the coming winter rains stopped campaigning. In February 1943, the Germans and their Italian Allies counterattacked at Kasserine Pass, breaking through the untried Americans. The attack was contained soon after, however, and the Axis forces escaped to the east back through Kasserine Pass on February 23.

The Americans put the experience of Kasserine to good use by improving training and command structure. In early March, Rommel attacked again at Medenine, but was repulsed after four unsuccessful assaults. Two weeks later a strong British offensive was launched at Mareth. The American II Corps was put back in the line and Gen. Eisenhower requested that they be given an active role. This time, the Americans would show themselves the equals of Rommel's seasoned troops.

Pvt. Minue is shown taking a position held by infantry of the German 90th Light Division in Tunisia on April 28, 1943. At age 44, he was well above the average age for an infantryman in 1943. He wears the M1 steel helmet introduced the previous year to replace the low-crowned M1917 helmet in use since World War I. The new pot-shaped helmet gave more protection to the soldier's ears and back of the head. His shirt is the olive-drab garrison shirt; it was made of sturdy, hard-wearing wool, as were the trousers. His boots are brown lace-up brogans, constructed with the rough side of the leather outermost. He wears the standard web field belt with combat straps (suspenders) and pouches for rifle ammunition. His weapon is the M1 Garand .30-cal. rifle, the first semi-automatic rifle adopted by the US Army.

C: Colonel Leon Johnson; Benghazi, Libya, August 1943

After a successful small raid in June 1942, the 9th Air Force organized a large raid against the Romanian town of Ploesti, the largest oil refinery complex under Axis control, which supplied one-third of the petroleum needs of the German Luftwaffe. Flying from bases in Tunisia, 178 B-24s began their 1,340-mile mission on August 1, 1943. The most controversial part of the plan was a low-level attack to avoid detection by Ploesti's formidable anti-aircraft defenses. Both in planning and execution, extreme care was taken to restrict damage to military targets in and around the town. Premature detonation of time-delay bombs, dense smoke, and jutting chimneys caused havoc amongst the attacking aircraft. In all, 54 B-24s were lost in the raid, which yielded an impressive five Medals of Honor.

One of the five Medals of Honor was presented to Colonel Leon Johnson, who had led the 44th Bombardment Group in the raid. Col. Johnson, shown at right, was on loan from 8th Air Force, whose patch he wears on the left upper arm of his M1941 field jacket. Due to the climate at the base in Benghazi, Col. Johnson is otherwise dressed in tropical kit. He wears a khaki cotton officer's overseas cap, with insignia of rank on the left front of the curtain. His shirt, tie, and trousers are also khaki, worn with smooth brown leather shoes with toecaps.

Col. Johnson stands in front of a B-24 Liberator of the 98th Bombardment Group. This aircraft, with nose art identifying it as the "Hail Columbia", was the aircraft of Colonel John "Killer" Kane, the figure at left. Col. Kane, who led the 98th in the raid, wears a light khaki cotton shirt of enlisted pattern, without shoulder straps, with the silver eagles of his rank on the collar. He wears the wings of a command pilot over his left pocket. His belt is the regulation web belt in khaki with a plain brass buckle. Col. Kane's more relaxed mode of dress reflects greater familiarity with the Tunisian climate.

D: Corporal Charles Kelly; Altavilla, Italy, September 1943

Corp. Charles Kelly is shown on the upper floor of a house which had earlier been converted into an ammunition storage area by the US Army. Several discarded weapons litter the floor, as Corp. Kelly resorts to dropping 60mm mortar shells on Germans approaching the house. Corp. Kelly had already fired a variety of weapons until all the ammunition was expended, including a BAR whose barrel had overheated. Thrown on the bed, it set the bedding on fire.

Kelly wears the M1941 "Parsons" jacket, constructed of cotton poplin material, treated to make it windproof. This jacket, although gradually supplanted by the M1944 field jacket, was a common item throughout the war. On his left shoulder he wears the patch of the 36th Infantry Division, an olive-drab "T" superimposed on a turquoise arrowhead. The trousers are made of dark olive-drab material, with slash pockets in the side seams, and bloused over light khaki leggings, laced up the outside. Corp. Kelly wears the standard web pistol belt with ammunition pouches for the M1 Garand's five-round clips.

Following the war Corp. Kelly, who had been the quintessential warrior, had great difficulties adjusting to the demands of peacetime life. Unrecognized at the time, Post-Traumatic Stress Disorder made readjustment to civilian life difficult for uncounted numbers of soldiers like "Commando" Kelly. The

This member of the 27th Infantry Division is sheltered in a foxhole on Saipan. He wears standard US web gear but has discarded the Parsons jacket and wool trousers in favor of cotton HBT shirt and trousers more suitable for the climate. (NARA)

In this photograph, a member of the 27th Division looks over a set of captured Japanese weapons and gear, including a highly coveted Samurai sword. Many soldiers would undertake extraordinary risks to pick up souvenirs of doubtful utility and orders had to be constantly published against looting. (NARA)

Baker's Company A, 105th Infantry Regiment came ashore with the rest of the 27th Division on June 16, 1944, the day after the initial landings conducted by the Marines.

Sometime on June 19, Sgt. Baker's company was pinned down when it came under heavy fire from Japanese automatic weapons. Seizing an opportunity, Sgt. Baker picked up a discarded bazooka and made his way to within 100yds of a Japanese machine gun nest. While under heavy fire, Sgt. Baker shot a rocket into the position, destroying the Japanese strongpoint. As the Japanese fire abated, the company returned to the assault and seized its objective.

Following the breaching of his defensive lines, General Y. Saito, the Japanese commander, realized that a successful defense of the island was no longer possible and ordered a last "Banzai Charge" in an effort to die with honor. The attack, when it came on July 7, hit with all the fury of desperation. Shouting cries of "Long live the Emperor" and "Ten thousand years!", approximately 3,000 Japanese troops struck the juncture between the 105th and the 165th regiments, driving deep wedges into

Sergeant Thomas Baker is shown in the everyday dress for warm climates such as the Pacific, consisting of a khaki cotton overseas cap, shirt, and tie. This official Army photograph has been heavily retouched by wartime censors to remove any distinguishing unit or branch of service insignia. (NARA)

man who had once been termed a "one-man Army" had the greatest of difficulties finding and maintaining a job, drifting from one small job to the next, often disappearing for weeks and even months at a time, in search of a solace that he would never find in civilian life. Pittsburgh's one-time favorite son was to be forgotten in his own lifetime by the nation that he had done so much to protect. In the words of the German novelist Erich Maria Remarque, "[e]ven those that survived the War were destroyed by it".

E: Sergeant Thomas Baker; Saipan, June 19, 1944

In June 1944, a combined Army and Marine force invaded Saipan, a rugged and hilly volcanic island in the central Pacific, to use as a base for long-range air operations against the Japanese mainland. The 27th Division was the Army component of the invasion force. Sergeant Thomas

The presentation of recently promoted Sergeant Charles "Commando" Kelly's Medal of Honor was conducted in Italy. Although the Army considered Kelly the first recipient of the Medal of Honor for ground combat in the European Theater of Operations, at least five awards had already been bestowed for ground combat in the invasion of Sicily. (NARA)

the defenders and, in some places, breaking the lines completely.

Early in the attack, Sgt. Baker was seriously wounded, yet refused evacuation. At this critical juncture, every man was needed to defend the perimeter. Despite a fierce defense, the Japanese managed to push to within five yards of the American position, and at this point, a comrade picked up the wounded Baker and began to carry him to the rear. When this soldier, too, was wounded, Sgt. Baker refused further evacuation, propped himself against a tree, and asked for the soldier's .45 Colt automatic pistol. With only eight rounds of ammunition, Sgt. Baker covered his company's retreat and when his body was found after the position was retaken, eight dead Japanese soldiers lay at his feet.

F: Sergeant Maynard Smith; over the English Channel, May 1, 1943

Sergeant Maynard Smith's first bombing mission started as a milk run to the target, the 20ft thick concrete U-boat pens at St. Nazaire in France. Over the target, however, intense flak and then German fighter aircraft soon brought down 25 percent of the attacking bombers. So severely damaged by flak that the pilot dared not risk evasive action, Sgt. Smith's B-17 was a raging inferno when he emerged from the belly turret. As he climbed out, he watched both waist gunners and the radio operator bail out. The left waist gunner snagged one of his parachute straps, however, and was left dangling at the open window. The fuselage in flames, Sgt. Smith walked over and asked the man if the heat were too much for him. It apparently was, for the man disentangled himself and jumped. For the next few hours, Sgt. Smith was left to attend to the fire, attacking German fighters, and a wounded tail gunner until the aircraft landed safely in England. None of the three men Sgt. Smith had watched bail out was ever seen again.

Sgt. Smith is wearing the AAF B-3 fleece-lined flying jacket with matching fleece-lined trousers and boots; a practical kit made necessary by the extremely cold temperatures at the attitudes at which US precision bombing was conducted. Due to the fire, his earphones were useless, as was the oxygen mask which he has discarded. Since all bombing missions over Germany required flying over water, he wears the yellow

rubberized Mae West life vest. The wounded tail gunner is wearing a variant of the B-3 jacket and a fleece-lined leather cap, which was particularly popular with enlisted air crew. Each crew position was provided with first-aid equipment, including morphine syringes, which Sgt. Smith has administered to the wounded man.

G: Sergeant Francis Currey; Malmedy, Belgium, December 21, 1944

Raised in the Catskill Mountains of New York, Private Francis Currey was a latter-day Sgt. Alvin York; he had spent his youth fishing and hunting small game and he put these skills to use when he found himself in the midst of one of the hardest fought actions in the Battle of the Bulge. Amid snow and ice, Sgt. Currey was suddenly facing the disguised tanks of SS Lt. Col. Otto Skorzeny, the man who had delighted Hitler by rescuing Mussolini in a lightning commando raid in September 1943.

In the extremely severe winter of 1944–45 in Northwest Europe, the American soldier was dressed very much like his World War I counterpart. Although special arctic clothing had been issued to the Army in the Aleutians and the Alaska Command, such clothing was not generally available in Europe. The overcoat, which was designed for dress as well as field wear, was a medium olive-drab with gold buttons. Although some times ordered removed for security reasons in the field, colored unit patches such as that of the 30th Division worn by Sgt. Currey were usually worn on the left sleeve. Supple mented with extra clothing

Abruptly taken off KP to attend his award ceremony, a class A tunic was found for Sgt. Smith, a pistol belt buckled around his waist, and he was rushed out to meet the US Secretary of War. When asked if he had a leave-pass for the night, Sgt. Smith said no, but he thought he could get one. (NARA)

underneath and a drab woolen muffler, the overcoat was the soldier's primary protection against the extreme cold.

The steel helmet was not designed with any thought for warmth; there was no difference between the helmets issued in the Pacific and those issued in the Arctic. Woolen knitted "Jeep caps" were often worn under the helmet liner for extra warmth. Long underwear was widely available to supplement the woolen trousers.

As in the Pacific, universal issue of one style of boot regardless of climate caused discomfort to the soldier in the field. Although it is true that special cold weather boots were in the supply system, they were not widely available in the Ardennes sector.

H: Private Carlton W. Barrett; Normandy, June 6, 1944

By early 1944, after the successful invasions of North Africa, Sicily, and Italy, the Western Allies prepared to take on Hitler's defenses in Northwest Europe. After much discussion as to the best location for invasion, the Allied High Command chose a stretch of sandy beach in Normandy.

The weather on June 6 was awful and many of the overburdened infantrymen were sea-sick as they piled into the "Higgins" boats for the final run to their assigned sectors. The landing site chosen for the 18th Regimental Combat Team was a 1,500yd stretch of beach, flanked by two small wooded draws that provided exits off the beach. Immediately behind these draws, approximately 500 to 1,000yds off the beach, were the initial objectives of the assault troops, the farming villages of Colleville-sur-Mer on the left flank and Saint-Laurent-sur-Mer on the right.

It was here, since nicknamed "Bloody Omaha", that Private Carlton W. Barrett waded ashore with the 18th Infantry Regiment of the US 1st Infantry Division. Confusion reigned all along the Omaha sector, as men and matériel piled up willy-nilly due to the nature of the landings themselves. Assigned as a guide, Pvt. Barrett was expected to move along the beach and point out the best routes across the beach to the advancing troops. He moved coolly along the beach under intense enemy fire and encouraged men by his example to get up and move off the beaches. Amidst the confusion, Barrett ran as a courier to take messages to the scattered commands. Darting back and forth along the fire-swept beach, Pvt. Barrett was an example to the demoralized men sheltered behind the low sea wall.

As new troops and additional supplies continued to arrive on the beach, adding yet further to the chaos, little attention was paid to the many wounded strewn on the beach. Pvt. Barrett, however, saw that many wounded men were in no position to make it to through the heavy surf, and he began carrying the wounded through the deep water and over the sand bar to waiting evacuation boats. Making numerous trips, under fire from enemy machine guns and mortars, Pvt. Barrett saved many men who would have otherwise perished.

For his numerous actions of bravery that day, Pvt. Barrett was one of four men awarded the Medal of Honor for the D-Day invasion.

Private Carlton Barrett, just awarded the Medal of Honor, is posed in this unusually introspective official Army photograph. He is wearing class A uniform and holds a presentation case with what appears to be an extra breast suspension ribbon, as well as the undress ribbon and rosette. Note the unusual suspension rig on the medal at his throat. (NARA)

INDEX